WORLD ATLAS

— OF —

TEA

WORLD ATLAS OF TEA

– KRISI SMITH –

FIREFLY BOOKS

A FIREFLY BOOK

Published by Firefly Books Ltd. 2016

First printing

Publisher Cataloging-in-Publication Data (U.S.)

Names: Smith, Krisi, author.
Title: World atlas of tea : from the leaf to the cup, the world's teas explored
      and enjoyed / Krisi Smith.
Description: Richmond Hill, Ontario, Canada : Firefly Books, 2016. | Includes
      index. | Summary: "This guidebook will take readers through the art of
      tea drinking, a journey from plants and their varieties to tea-brewing
      techniques, tea blending, and finally profiles on several tea-prominent
      countries" -- Provided by publisher.
Identifiers: ISBN 978-1-77085-816-9 (hardcover)
Subjects: LCSH: Tea. | Cooking (Tea)
Classification: LCC SB271.S658 |DDC 641.3372 – dc23

Library and Archives Canada Cataloguing in Publication

Smith, Krisi, author
        World atlas of tea : from the leaf to the cup, the world's teas explored
and enjoyed / Krisi Smith.
Includes index.
ISBN 978-1-77085-816-9 (hardback)
        1. Tea. 2. Tea trade. I. Title.
GT2905.S65 2016   641.3'372   C2016-902861-5

Published in the United States by
Firefly Books (U.S.) Inc.
P.O. Box 1338, Ellicott Station
Buffalo, New York 14205

Published in Canada by
Firefly Books Ltd.
50 Staples Avenue, Unit 1
Richmond Hill, Ontario L4B 0A7

Printed and bound in China

> To Mike and my amazing team at Bluebird, who remind me on a daily basis that everything is possible.

First published in Great Britain by Mitchell Beazley, a division of Octopus Publishing Group Ltd
Carmelite House, 50 Victoria Embankment London EC4Y 0DZ

The publishers will be grateful for any information that will assist them in keeping future editions up to date. Although all reasonable care has been taken in the preparation of this book, neither the publishers nor the author can accept any liability for any consequence arising from the use thereof, or the information contained therein. Every effort has been made to trace copyright holders and to obtain their permission for the use of copyright material. The publisher apologizes for any errors or omissions and would be grateful if notified of any corrections that should be incorporated in future editions of this book.

Publisher Denise Bates; **Art Director** Juliette Norsworthy; **Senior Editor** Alex Stetter; **Designer** Lizzie Ballantyne; **Special Photography** Cristian Barnett; **Illustrator** Grace Helmer; **Copy Editor** Jane Birch **Picture Research Manager** Giulia Hetherington; **Picture Researcher** Jennifer Veall; **Production Controller** Allison Gonsalves; **Cartography** Digital mapping by Encompass Graphics Ltd,Hove, UK, www.encompass-graphics.co.uk

CONTENTS

INTRODUCTION

There has never been a more exciting time to discover, or rather rediscover, our much-loved cup of tea. Innovative new ideas, cultures and concepts are shaking up long-standing traditions in the tea industry, from farming methods and blending techniques to the type of tea ware we use and the social occasions at which tea plays a central role.

The question is no longer "One lump of sugar or two?" but rather "What variety of tea would you like to drink today?" Green, black or even raspberry leaf, perhaps? Would you like your tea served hot with milk, shaken over ice or steamed into a frothy chai latte?

It's no secret that the trend for good-quality coffee has exploded into our lives over the past few years and the same is now happening for tea. Moving from a mass-market commodity that we consume without giving it a second thought to a method of discovery and part of our wider well-being, tea is becoming part of how we define ourselves. We care more and more about where it has come from, how it has been processed and what tools we use to prepare it.

The way a humble cup of tea can improve a bad day or soothe frayed nerves is part of why I chose to make my living in the tea industry. But the ability to spread delight, joy and excitement through innovative blending or flavorful tea mixology is a relatively recent phenomenon and it is one I am passionate about being a part of. I first noticed this change in attitude and approach to tea a few years ago when I was working for an innovative tea blender in North America. Once I had been introduced to this vibrant and varied new world of tea, there was no going back.

In 2012 I moved back home to England and set up my own tea company, Bluebird Tea Co. Every day I get to create with tea, share it with others and watch as such a simple thing brings happiness to someone's day. It is an exciting industry to be working in at this time and I am delighted to be introducing it to you in this book.

Now is very much the time for tea.

Opposite: Tea is enjoyed in a variety of different ways around the world. In India, spiced black tea, or chai, is traditionally served very milky and very sweet.

Photographed in May 1938, two young women enjoy a refreshing cup of tea while perched on the diving board of a public swimming pool in Finchley, North London.

PART ONE

TEA BASICS

THE TEA PLANT

Most people are surprised to learn that all types of tea are from the same plant: *Camellia sinensis*, a species of evergreen bush native to Asia. There are two main varieties used for cultivation: *Camellia sinensis* var. *assamica* and *Camellia sinensis* var. *sinensis*, each of which thrives under different conditions and produces unique-tasting teas. There is also a more common variety — *Camellia sinensis* var. *japonica* — that will happily grow in most backyards, but is not as well suited to drinking.

The tea plant can grow in most climates, but it is mostly cultivated in subtropical and tropical climates where the conditions produce the most desirable tea. First discovered in China, the *Camellia sinensis* plant was spread throughout Asia by Buddhist monks who drank tea for both medicinal and spiritual purposes. For many years the oldest record of cultivated tea plants in China was dated around 3000 BCE. However, fossilized tea roots recently discovered in China's Zhejiang Province show signs of cultivation dating thousands of years earlier — to nearly 7000 BCE. It was only in the 1600s that the tea plant was cultivated further afield, in countries such as India, Sri Lanka and Kenya, with the purpose of producing black tea for the British and Dutch Empires.

Since these ancient and humble beginnings, tea has become a global phenomenon and part of billions of people's daily lives. To feed this demand tea is now grown in over 35 countries worldwide, producing over 3.3 billion tons (3 billion tonnes) of tea for consumption each year.

GROWING WILD

When thinking of the tea plant, most people envision terraces of neatly pruned, green bushes defining the landscape as far as the eye can see. However, in its natural, uncultivated form, the evergreen tea shrub can actually resemble a medium-sized tree, 13 to 55 ft. (4–17 m) tall, with gangly branches and a wide canopy. It is interesting to note that it is uncertain if any truly wild plants still exist, as even those found in the most remote places are presumed to be a result of previous cultivation.

The *assamica* variety tends to grow taller and has a more "treelike" appearance, while all *Camellia sinensis* plants have deep roots, a thin trunk and many branches which produce leaves as well as fruit and small flowers. There are subtle differences in the leaves of the tea plant, depending on variety, but most are about 3.5 in. (8 cm) long with slightly serrated edges, shiny, dark emerald green in color and leathery to the touch. *Assamica* has darker, larger and more shiny leaves.

PESTS AND DISEASES

The tea plant's most common pests are mites and aphids, which cause the leaves to turn yellow and often to fall off. The most common diseases that threaten the tea plant are fungus- and bacteria-based diseases, such as dieback and canker, as well as root rot and blister blight, which can severely damage or even kill the plant. In many tea-growing areas fungicides are used to protect the plants (see page 16).

The flowers of a tea plant are approximately 1.25 in. (3 cm) in size, white with a light-yellow pollen; its fruit is brownish-green and contains seeds that help germinate new plants. This hardy plant can live up to 50 years in most terrains and has relatively few pests and diseases compared to other plants.

Thea bohea.

ASSAMICA VERSUS SINENSIS

There is a clear preference in terrain, climate and rainfall for each strain of tea plant. These differences in growing conditions cause a change in not only the plant's outward appearance but also go on to play a big role in determining which harvesting and processing methods are used to get the preferred yield, type and quality of the resulting tea.

Camellia sinensis bushes are cultivated in cool, high-altitude terraces across Asia, where the changing seasons on the mountainside produce a small, lush, sweet leaf that is full of fragrant flavor. These characteristics make the *sinensis* plants perfect for producing fragrant green, white and oolong teas, but they are sometimes used to produce black tea, too. In many areas there is no harvesting over the winter months so the first pluck of spring, or first flush, is often renowned as the most flavorful.

Assamica bushes are better suited to hotter, tropical climates with at least 80 in. (200 cm) of annual rainfall, as found in the northern hill stations of India and Yunnan Province in China. With consistent climate and terrain, *assamica* plants produce regrowth within weeks of being plucked, so they are usually harvested repeatedly throughout the year. That said, there is still a preference for teas plucked during spring (first flush in particular) or after the monsoons.

For many companies wanting to produce large amounts of black tea for the mainstream market, *assamica* is the obvious choice because of its greater yield potential and more resilient leaves. These larger, robust leaves are perfect for the more vigorous processing required to create black teas as well as some types of teas that require more complicated or lengthy processing, such as pu'erh, oolong or smoked teas (see page 23).

CULTIVATION

For the purpose of cultivation both varieties of tea plant are pruned to a much more manageable size than the wild plants (see page 13) for harvesting, usually no more than arm's-reach wide and no higher than waist height. Regular pruning also encourages a higher yield of young leaves and buds, which are ideal for tea production, so it is rare to see any flowers or fruit on a cultivated tea plant.

Camellia sinensis plants are resilient and can grow in most climates and soils. However, to produce the highest quality teas, they need moist, deep, acidic soil together with a warm, humid climate above 50°F (10°C) and at least 40 in. (100 cm) of annual rainfall.

A wet and misty climate allows the leaves to mature slowly in warm, moist conditions while being sheltered from the harsh sunlight, which is why most of the world's highest quality tea-growing regions are also at an altitude above 4,000 ft. (1,200 m). The leaves absorb a high amount of water, too, so they remain lush and tender, developing exceptional flavor.

Tea plants take 3 to 5 years to mature so it is common practice for estates to have their own small nursery field where seedlings are nurtured for 2 to 3 years before being planted out in the tea fields on the wider estate. Cuttings are taken from healthy, mature tea plants and the soil is painstakingly turned, weeded and watered to ensure the seedlings' roots can take hold and draw up the moisture and nutrients they need to survive. Once mature, the young bushes are planted in rows, much like any other agricultural product, and, if on a steep mountainside, often on specially prepared terraces — stepped, narrow strips cut into the sides of slopes to make the most of the land available. These terraces also have built-in irrigation channels to manage and maximize the rainfall, bringing water to every plant.

Opposite: A view of a tea plantation and temple at Horse Head Rock in the Wuyi Mountains, Fujian Province, China. The Wuyi Mountains have a long history of *Assamica* cultivation.

Below: Tea gardens at Munnar, a hill station in the Western Ghats mountain range of Kerala, India. Grown at high altitude across Asia, *Camellia sinensis* thrives in cool temperatures.

ORGANIC VERSUS PESTICIDES

Many tea estates and farms use fertilizers and pesticides to enhance both yield and quality of tea, but the main reason for using pesticides is to prevent outbreaks of pests or diseases that could wipe out entire crops. In some countries, such as Japan, the use of pesticides and fertilizers is common practice and seen as the norm, necessary to enable a consistently high-quality harvest. In other countries such as Sri Lanka, there is a commitment to growing "clean" tea using natural fertilizer such as manure and off-cuts from the plants themselves, but a base level of pesticides is still used to help with pest control. Copper fungicides are commonly used, for example, to prevent and control blister blight, a common tea plant disease. Organic farming, or farming without the use of any chemical pesticides or fertilizers, is often perceived to be the ideal, and with the right growing conditions, knowledge and effective management, organic farming can produce fantastic teas. It is also fair to say that reckless use of pesticides can harm both the environment and those later consuming the produce. However, organically farming tea it is a complex, multilayered issue with no simple conclusion.

The biggest problem is lack of education around safe practice, which can result in harmful overuse of pesticides and overfarming that can damage the environment and biodiversity irrevocably. Effects of using pesticides and of overfarming can include human diseases, destruction of the natural organisms of the soil, pollution of both environment and water supply — affecting humans and animals — damaging biodiversity and causing soil erosion.

A healthy tea bush can be cultivated in most tea-growing countries with little more than a decent water supply, a good compost and soil base and healthy biodiversity. Remember, tea cultivation has been around for thousands of years, whereas fertilizers are only a recent development. But there are a variety of reasons why pesticides and fertilizers are used and each must be considered in the context of the environment in which they are used.

In some areas of the world, such as in Assam in India, it wouldn't be possible economically for small-scale tea farmers to meet demand without the help of fertilizers, as they allow farmers to double their yield with less land, work and cost. As the tea market gets more competitive, fertilizers and pesticides also play a huge role in ensuring a high, consistent quality of tea. With the tea industry driving the economy and providing jobs for whole regions, in what are often poor rural areas, it would be harsh and unrealistic to expect farmers to stop using these enhancements without providing viable alternatives, and often the switch to expensive organic fertilizers is just not economically sustainable.

In Japan, the use of pesticides and fertilizers is common practice, to the extent that is it nearly impossible for tea farmers to switch to organic farming, even if they wished to. Alongside the practical issues of time and money, those who wish to set up organic farms are denied the resources, equipment and support from the wider industry and farming community. The biggest barrier to organic farming in Japan is space. An organic farm cannot be established near land where any fertilizers are used without an adequate buffer zone, and nonorganic farmers do not want organic plants near their land as they tend to attract more wildlife, meaning they have to spend more on their own fertilizers. The challenges are huge.

Considering the reasoning behind the use of fertilizers and pesticides may help us understand motives, but it still doesn't change the reality that irresponsible use can have devastating effects on the environment as a whole.

COOKING WITH TEA

A great source of vitamins, minerals and antioxidants, tea leaves have been used in cooking for hundreds of years in the Far East. A simple way of using tea leaves in your own cooking is adding them to stock or soup much like you would a bay leaf, allowing them to simmer and add flavor. You can also add them to stir-fries or rice dishes, serve them raw as part of a wild salad or try them battered in a tempura-style recipe.

GROWING YOUR OWN TEA

You may be surprised to learn that you don't need a tropical hill station to grow your own tea plants. In fact, a variety of *Camellia sinensis* var. *japonica* is readily available in most garden centers and, with a little TLC, will happily grow in your own back garden.

First, decide if you wish to grow your tea plants from seeds or cuttings (this is more difficult) or purchase a young seedling or a mature plant (a much easier option). If you wish to plant outside immediately and are keen to harvest leaves to use in cooking, then start with an adult plant if possible, as seeds and cuttings take 3 to 5 years to mature.

GROWING FROM SEED

1. Plant up to five seeds, spaced approximately 1.25 in. (3 cm) apart, in a pot at least 6 in. (15 cm) in diameter that has plenty of drainage holes. You should use slightly acidic potting soil (pH 5 is best) or ericaceous compost.

2. Place the pot in a warm, sunny spot that is partially shaded, for example in a greenhouse or on a windowsill.

3. Repot your plant into a larger pot as it grows to ensure that its roots have enough room.

4. Once your tea plant is over 20 in. (50 cm) high and/or 2 years old, it will survive quite happily in your yard. It will need a bright, sunny spot and acidic soil to thrive (see "Growing young or mature plants" →).

PROPAGATING FROM CUTTINGS

1. Use a healthy, mature tea plant to take a cutting. Look for a stem with both a healthy leaf and bud forming. Cut the stem at an angle, about 1.5 in. (4 cm) below a leaf node (forming bud), with pruning shears or a sharp knife.

2. Fill a well-drained pot with half ericaceous compost or acidic soil and half potting soil, then water well.

3. Using a toothpick, make a hole in the soil and insert the cutting into it as deep as it will go, without letting the leaf touch the soil.

4. Keep the cutting moist and warm, either in a mini greenhouse or by placing the pot on a windowsill and covering it with a clear plastic bag secured with a rubber band. If using the latter option, be sure to remove the plastic bag for 2 to 5 hours every day to allow fresh air to circulate around the cutting.

5. After 10 weeks the cutting should have firm roots and be producing new growth, at which point you can repot.

6. Once your tea plant is over 20 in. (50 cm) high and/or 2 years old, it will survive quite happily in your yard. It will need a bright, sunny spot and acidic soil to thrive (see "Growing young or mature plants" below).

GROWING YOUNG OR MATURE PLANTS

1. Find a warm, sunny spot in your yard that isn't in direct sunlight all day.

2. The soil needs to be acidic — at pH 5 or less. You can use a soil-testing kit, available from garden centers, to check the acidity of your soil. If your soil is not acidic enough, then better options are planting in a container or a raised bed filled with ericaceous compost.

3. If winter temperatures drop below 14°F (-10°C), you might want to consider bringing your plant under cover or protecting it with horticultural fleece.

Left: To thrive, tea seedlings need a well-lit, warm spot that is shaded for part of the day. Repot them into larger containers as they grow so that the roots are not constrained.

Some members of the tea family are valued for their blossoms rather than their leaves: cultivated in China for over a thousand years, *Camellia sinensis* var. *japonica* was introduced to Europe in the 16th century, adding welcome color to gardens in early spring.

THE CHEMISTRY OF TEA

The chemical composition of tea is fairly complex, with thousands of compounds found in both the plant and the leaf itself. Some compounds go through chemical reactions, breaking down or combining to form new compounds during growing and processing stages, and some change again when infused in hot water. Because processing methods have such an effect on the chemical make-up of tea, different types of tea have different chemical make-ups, too. It is the combined effect of these many compounds and reactions that creates the unique aromas, tastes and mouthfeel that we experience when drinking our favorite tea.

The main compounds found in a tea leaf are:

POLYPHENOLS

These are the most common and the most influential of the chemical compounds found in a tea leaf. Polyphenols help the plant fight off pests and diseases, especially useful for the younger, more vulnerable, leaves and shoots.

Among the polyphenols in tea are flavonoids, which are broken down during oxidization (see page 47) and then join with other molecules to create theaflavins and thearubigins, which are responsible for the darker color and stronger flavors that develop during oxidization. Other flavonoids such as catechin are important as they are thought to be responsible for not for only taste and color but also antioxidants.

ENZYMES

Enzymes play an important role in the processing of tea leaves, in particular the oxidization stage, which is an enzymatic reaction that causes both the color and the flavor of the leaves to change (see page 47).

This reaction can be halted by applying heat, which is why leaves are dried following oxidization and why the first stage of green tea production is usually to apply heat — a process known as "killing the green" (see page 52).

AMINO ACIDS

Amino acids are present in tea in many forms but theanine is the most prominent. Amino acids are converted to polyphenols when the plant is exposed to sunlight. Interestingly, some teas, such as matcha, are shaded for the last few weeks before harvesting to encourage a higher number of amino acids. It is the theanine compounds, in particular L-theanine, that are said to have a positive effect on your mind when absorbed into the body alongside the caffeine molecules — an effect described as a relaxed uplift but with no crash later, as can happen when you absorb caffeine from coffee.

THEARUBIGINS

As a result of oxidization, catechins are converted into thearubigins. Because of the high level of oxidization that takes place in the production of black teas in particular, between 60 and 70 percent of this type of tea is made up of thearubigins. They are also sometimes referred to as tannins and affect changes in color and taste, usually making the tea darker and more astringent.

CARBOHYDRATES

Just like other plants, the tea plant stores energy as carbohydrates, which it generates through photosynthesis. The tea plant can then draw upon these stores to fuel important reactions in the tea leaves, both while the plant is growing and also later during processing.

MINERALS

A variety of minerals are found in tea leaves, including selenium, aluminum, fluorine, potassium, zinc, magnesium and iodine, which have different effects on the human body. Among the most notable is fluorine, which can help maintain healthy teeth. Mineral content of tea leaves varies depending on growing conditions as well as the type and age of the leaves being processed.

VOLATILE FLAVOR AND AROMA COMPOUNDS

There are many flavor and aroma compounds in tea, and these volatile substances combine to create a complex structure that is responsible for the subtle tasting notes and scents that you enjoy in your favorite cup. Some are responsible for bitterness, some sweetness, whereas others give the tea roasted scents or brisk flavors.

CAFFEINE

Caffeine is a natural stimulant found in tea leaves, created by the tea plant as a form of protection against bugs and pests (see also page 101). Caffeine can affect your heart rate, brain waves and physical function, both positively and negatively. Just like minerals, the caffeine levels found in tea leaves can vary depending on the climate and terrain, the species of the plant and the type of leaves being processed.

The main chemical reactions that take place in a tea leaf are:

PHOTOSYNTHESIS

This is the process whereby the plant creates and stores energy as carbohydrates while it grows in the sunlight. These carbohydrates help along the enzymatic process during oxidization later and help convert amino acids into polyphenols.

WITHERING

Water compounds are lost from the leaf as soon as they are plucked from the plant and begin to wilt. The cell walls of the leaf break down, too (see also page 46).

OXIDIZATION

As cell walls begin to break down, the chemistry of the leaf changes as the compounds go through an enzymatic reaction with the oxygen molecules in the air. The main chemical change is the flavonoids converting to theaflavins (see also page 20).

Below: Tea leaves are laid out on the cool factory floor to oxidize in this image from a Ceylon (now Sri Lanka) tea plantation, which dates from about 1910.

VARIETIES, BLENDS AND GRADES

There can be some confusion between varieties of tea, tea grades and tea blends. For our purposes, when discussing **tea varieties** we are referring to the different forms the tea leaf can take after processing, such as green, black, white and so on.

Tea grades refer to the grade of leaf plucked from the tea plant, or the particle size once processed. Certain grades of leaf are better suited to certain varieties of tea. For example, most white tea is processed from the buds or shoots of the tea plant, which is the highest grade of tea leaf.

Finally, use of the term **tea blends** refers to the beverages that are made from a mixture of different tea leaves and other ingredients.

Once grown, harvested and processed, different varieties of tea, from white and green to black and pu'erh, can be further graded based upon quality or strength of flavor. These teas can be enjoyed on their own or the leaves may be mixed with other ingredients to create an infinite number of tea blends. It is also popular to scent tea leaves, during the processing or blending stages, to create unique aromas, such as jasmine tea (see page 107 for more about this). There are many more varieties of infusion that are made from plants and herbs other than the *Camellia sinensis* plant — these are referred to as tisanes or herbal teas (see page 33).

TEA VARIETIES

WHITE TEA

White tea is the least processed tea variety: the tea leaves are often just plucked and then gently dried. The ideal leaves to use are the top few, or even just the shoots, usually hand-plucked in the first harvests of the year. White tea is mainly produced in the Far East, most famously in the Chinese province of Fujian but also in Taiwan and Sri Lanka. White teas are light in color, sometimes downy to the touch and often still "leafy" in appearance. They tend to be the most delicate in taste and aroma, and go well with high fragrant notes such as rose or jasmine. As a general rule, white teas are nutrient rich and low in caffeine. However, this is not always the case: some premium white teas, such as Silver Needle, have caffeine levels similar to those of green tea, as the young shoots produce caffeine as they grow, as a form of pest deterrent.

GREEN TEA

Green tea is uniquely processed as it goes through an additional drying stage in order to halt oxidization (see page 52). This preserves its green, leafy appearance and its antioxidant levels, as well as inhibiting the development of caffeine. Because of this, green teas have been hailed as the healthy tea of choice.

Historically, green tea was the first variety to be developed and today it is produced in large quantities in both China and Japan. Different countries use their own drying methods: some pan-roast whereas others steam, giving each green tea a unique flavor and appearance. Green tea is one of the most versatile of teas, with over 200 varieties. Some green teas are also rolled into tight balls, called pellets or pearls, which unfurl when brewed. Most green teas go well with citrus flavors, roasted notes and light floral or honey fragrances.

OOLONG TEA

This tea variety is, uniquely, partially oxidized and often rolled. Oolong teas share some characteristics with both green and black teas — they have light flavor notes but are often more complex in taste than green teas, but not as strong as black teas. The best oolong teas are traditionally from Taiwan and can be re-steeped up to eight times. Oolong leaves are distinctively curled, twisted or balled, with a slight gray-green or blue-green hue.

BLACK TEA

Black tea is the most common tea variety, making up 90 percent of tea consumed in the Western world and rapidly catching up with green tea elsewhere, too. Black teas are fully oxidized so are dark brown in color and higher in caffeine that other tea varieties. The leaves themselves are smaller and thinner than other varieties and can sometimes be cut into smaller particles, which resemble granules. Black teas have a great depth of flavor and are usually enjoyed with milk.

PU'ERH TEA

Pu'erh is the whiskey of the tea world — it is aged and complex. Traditionally produced in the Chinese province of Yunnan, pu'erh tea leaves are packed into cakes or bricks to mature over time. When the tea is ready to drink, small quantities can be crumbled from the cake or brick, for each cup at a time. Pu'erh teas have a wonderful combination of flavor and aroma notes, often similar to malt, chocolate or coffee but with a light freshness that is associated with green teas.

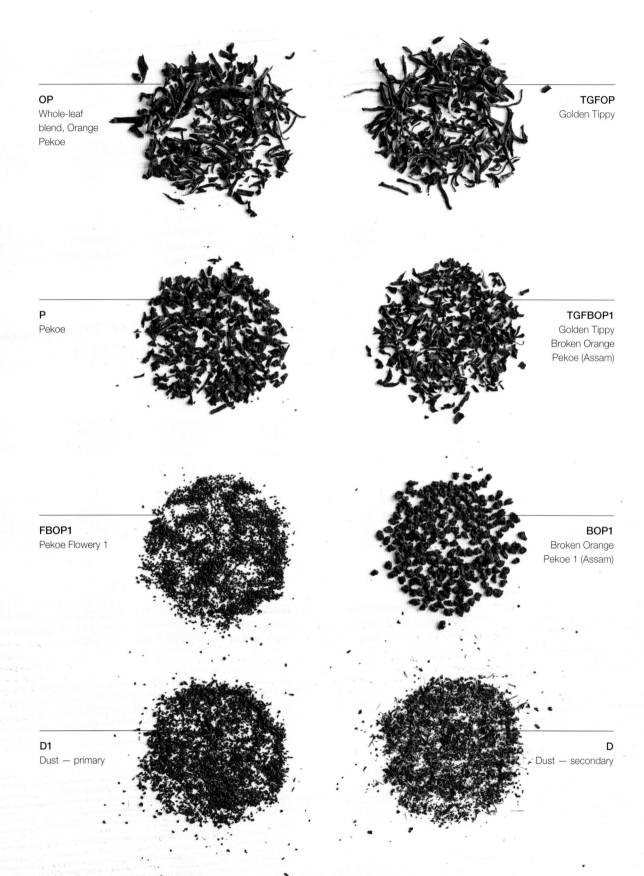

OP
Whole-leaf
blend, Orange
Pekoe

TGFOP
Golden Tippy

P
Pekoe

TGFBOP1
Golden Tippy
Broken Orange
Pekoe (Assam)

FBOP1
Pekoe Flowery 1

BOP1
Broken Orange
Pekoe 1 (Assam)

D1
Dust — primary

D
Dust — secondary

TEA GRADES

Tea grades are used to differentiate between leaf size and shape, as well as where on the plant the leaf was plucked from. Grading takes place at the last stage of processing, where the tea is sifted through mesh to filter it according to leaf-particle size (see page 55). Larger leaves or those from higher up on the plant are not necessarily better, but these qualities do affect the flavors of the final tea produced. Tea grades can be helpful in order to help price the tea in the market with "higher" grades being an indicator of quality, though this isn't always the case.

The lack of a universal grading system can make it difficult to understand tea grades and their roles in the industry. Some countries, such as China, use numbers, whereas others, such as Japan, use region and harvest dates. Still others use descriptive words, which can be confusing. The grading system developed by the British-run plantations in India and Sri Lanka in the 19th century, which uses letters such as BOP (Broken Orange Pekoe), is perhaps the most commonly recognized, and is still used today for most black tea production.

THE "BRITISH" SYSTEM

In countries like Sri Lanka that have a rich history of producing black teas for export, the grading system is based upon letters that stand for certain terms. The grades fall into three overarching categories: "whole leaf," "broken leaf" and "CTC (Crush, Tear, Curl) leaves" and are not necessarily considered in terms of quality, but rather by size of leaf. Bigger leaves, say Pekoe grade, are higher up the grading system and would make a light but fragrant tea. Smaller broken-leaf grades like BOPF (Broken Orange Pekoe Fannings) may still be as good in terms of quality

ORTHODOX VERSUS CTC

Once processed, the tea leaves are described as "orthodox," which refers to the whole leaf, or the particles of whole leaf. However, the factory may wish to cut the tea at the final stage of processing. This involves cutting and tearing the leaves into smaller particles, which are then rolled and curled into pellet-type particles. This is helpful if you want to produce strong, malty black teas that are usually taken with milk. The increased surface area of the smaller particles ensures that the cup is full of flavor and the infusion time is reduced, making it perfect for higher-quality teabags, too. Once cut, the tea is referred to as CTC, or Crush, Tear, Curled.

ORTHODOX GRADES, "BRITISH" SYSTEM

Countries that use this grading system include India, Sri Lanka and Kenya. The following abbreviations are commonly used:

T — Tippy: tips are present, indicates high quality due to the leaves being plucked from the very tips of the tea plant **GF — Golden Flowery:** indicates a golden hue to some or all of the leaves, a mark of high quality as this color is found at the tips of young shoots and buds plucked during the first flushes of the season **F — Finest:** used to indicate the highest level of the grade in question

Grades listed in order, starting with the highest grade:

OP — Orange Pekoe: full, whole leaves
FBOP — Flowery Broken Orange Pekoe: broken whole leaves consisting of large particles and perhaps some tips
BOP1 — Broken Orange Pekoe 1: broken whole leaves of medium particle size, often twisted in appearance
Pekoe: broken, curled leaf of medium particle size
BOP — Broken Orange Pekoe: small particles of leaf
BOPF — Broken Orange Pekoe Fannings: smaller particles still than BOP
Dust 1: fine particles, almost dustlike in appearance

CTC GRADES, "BRITISH" SYSTEM

BP1 — Broken Pekoe: the largest CTC particle, great flavor
PF1 — Pekoe Fanning: darker, grainy particles, slightly smaller than BP1
PD — Pekoe Dust: fine particles with body
D1 — Dust: very small particles, the most strength
D — Dust: very small particles made from broken leaves
BMF — Broken Mixed Fannings: high content of fibers, little tea leaf present

as the Pekoe, but its smaller leaf particles would make a much darker, stronger tea.

Dust, the lowest grade, or smallest particle size, can contain fragments from leaves of various sizes and also of veins and stems. It is the easiest and the cheapest to produce but, rather than being considered low-quality, dust can actually be the most desirable "strong, dark" tea, sought after for export by many European countries.

SINGLE-ESTATE TEAS

Tea leaves grown in a single location and often plucked during the same harvest are known as single-estate teas. Usually grown on specialized estates, these teas are synonymous with both good quality and premium price tags.

The concept is similar to that of good-quality wine, where grapes grown in one vineyard are used to produce a wine variety, often of the same name. Each vineyard aims for its name to become known for the quality and uniqueness of its grapes. Much like their wine counterparts, tea connoisseurs enjoy exploring and developing their tastes to discover their favorite tea estates and year of harvest.

It is easy to see how these single-estate teas gain their luxury price tags when you consider they are usually handpicked and often have only a few weeks per season with the perfect harvesting conditions. A few weeks of bad weather, as well as other risk factors such as pests, disease or labor strikes, could wipe out a whole harvest. This is why it is much safer for most commercial tea companies to hedge their bets and create a blend of teas from various origins, sometimes up to 40 different locations.

WELL-KNOWN SINGLE-ESTATE TEAS

Some of the best-known single-estate teas are:
Darjeeling — from Darjeeling, India
Assam — from Assam, India
White Silver Needle (Bai Hao Yin Zhen) — from Fujian Province, China
Gyokuro — from Uji, Japan
Dragon Well — from Zhejiang Province, China

Tea pickers pluck leaves on the
Makaibari Tea Estate in Kurseong, Darjeeling,
India, first established in the 1850s.
In 2014 its Silver Tips Imperial tea, a light
oolong, became the most expensive
Indian tea ever sold.

TEA BLENDS

A tea blend simply refers to a mixture of two or more types of tea, or other ingredients, that are mixed together to produce a desired taste. There are countless varieties of tea blends out there, with new ones being created all the time by tea companies searching for the next great blend.

Sometimes tea blends are also scented, often with floral notes such as rose or jasmine (as we will explore later — see page 107), and they can be mixed with ingredients other than the tea plant, such as herbs or flowers. Perhaps the most famous tea blends are English breakfast and masala chai, and among the most famous scented tea blends are jasmine tea and Earl Grey.

ENGLISH BREAKFAST

English breakfast tea is typically blended using three or more varieties of black tea, often from different countries, usually from northern India, Sri Lanka, Kenya, Rwanda and the Chinese Province of Yunnan. As the name suggests, this tea blend was developed by the British to suit their tastes and diet — a tea to be taken with milk and enjoyed with dense, sweet foods, such as cakes or scones. Unsurprisingly, the tea plantations that are geared up to produce these types of tea are in countries that were once part of the British Empire and were established during the colonial era.

MASALA CHAI

The word *chai* means "tea" in many Asian and Indian languages and *masala* means "a mixture of spices." A masala chai is a tea blend made from a mixture of Indian black tea leaves and spices such as peppercorns, ginger, cardamom and cinnamon. It is traditionally prepared in a big pan of milk, with the tea leaves, spices and plenty of sugar, slowly boiled on a stove (see page 119).

EARL GREY

Earl Grey is made from black tea, usually a milder tasting leaf produced in China, India or Sri Lanka, and scented with oil from the bergamot plant. Bergamot is native to Southeast Asia but was later introduced to Europe, where it is produced commercially to be used across the perfume industry as well as to scent tea.

The natural oil is extracted from the fruit of the bergamot plant, which is similar to an orange — its light, citrus notes are well suited to scenting tea — although if you use too much you can end up with the "soapy" taste sometimes associated with Earl Grey tea blends.

Both the name of the tea and its widespread popularity are credited to Earl Grey, Prime Minister of Britain during the 1830s, who is said to have developed a taste for it after visiting China.

Ingredients used in chai include (clockwise from the top) peppercorns, star anise, cardamom, cinnamon, cloves and (center) black tea leaves.

EARL GREY MYTHS

Many myths surrounding the origin of this tea blend exist, including one that Charles Grey, 2nd Earl Grey, was gifted the first Earl Grey blend by a Chinese aristocrat after saving either the aristocrat or his son, depending on which version you read. However, this is unlikely as the bergamot plant wasn't known in China in the 1800s. It is more probable that the Earl developed a taste for scented teas while in China on a diplomatic visit, where scented teas were very popular at the time and that, upon his return to Britain, he sought out further scented teas to enjoy. Bergamot would have been readily available in Britain as it was used in perfumery. Another myth suggests that the scenting was accidental, the result of the tea leaves being stored next to bergamot oranges during a shipment from Asia to the Earl's estate. It is also possible that the scented tea was developed to be sold to the lower classes, perhaps as a way of disguising lower-quality tea or masking bad-tasting water, and named after the Earl as a clever marketing ploy by a 19th-century tea company.

Charles Grey, 2nd Earl Grey (1764–1845)

JASMINE TEA

This is one of the most famous scented teas. Originating in China's Fujian Province, jasmine tea is created by laying jasmine flowers on, or next to, freshly plucked tea leaves. Tea leaves will happily absorb aromas around them (which is why you need to store your tea leaves in an airtight container — see page 93), so they gradually begin to carry the light floral aroma. The jasmine blossoms can be removed before the tea leaves are dried and blended, or they can be left in to further add to the scent, flavor and appearance of the blend. Jasmine can be used to scent all forms of tea but it is typically used to scent white and green teas as they are light enough to balance with the delicate aroma, as well as serving as a good stomach- and nerve-settler. Jasmine pearls are also a much-loved jasmine tea blend (see the box on page 32).

FLOWERING TEA

One of the most beautiful of all teas, flowering tea, sometimes also called blooming tea, involves the highly skilled practice of hand-tying and -rolling tea leaves and flower blossoms into an arrangement that looks like a flower in full bloom. The tea is cleverly tied into a sphere, approximately 2 in. (5 cm) in diameter, which is wrapped in simple tea leaves, either white or green. When placed in hot water, the sphere magically opens up to reveal the flower inside. Blooming tea is traditionally Chinese and usually contains scented green or white tea leaves.

AFTERNOON TEA

This is the name of a tea blend taken as part of a much-loved social tradition, established by 17th-century London high society, consisting of a light meal accompanied by tea to ward off hunger between lunch and a late dinner engagement. As a general rule, afternoon tea blends are black tea-based, light and uplifting and must complement the light foods enjoyed at teatime. They must also be able to take milk and sugar, so a crisp, balanced black tea like Ceylon is commonly used. Sometimes afternoon tea blends are scented with floral notes like rose or jasmine to reflect their high-society, "English tea garden" origins.

The importance that the ritual of tea drinking came to hold in Europe is depicted in this painting of 1778, entitled *Afternoon Tea*, by Flemish painter Jan Anton Garemijn (1712–99).

PEARLS AND GUNPOWDER

You may have come across some rather unusual tea names — this comes from a deep tradition of using very literal names for tea. For example, pearled tea, such as jasmine pearls or dragon pearls, are so named because the leaves' appearance is similar to the size and shape of pearls. The tea leaves are hand-rolled, and often hand-tied, into little pearl-sized balls that delicately unravel when brewed — it is a beautiful sight! The careful hand-rolling and hand-tying are also indicators of the tea's luxurious and special nature.

Gunpowder tea is similarly named because the tiny rolled pellets of green tea resemble gunpowder.

Although the aesthetic beauty of rolled tea is not to be ignored, there are much more practical reasons for rolling leaves into these shapes. The first reason is that the shape can be more easily stored and transported.

The second, and more important, reason is that rolling leaves into balls seals in the flavors and aromas that have developed throughout processing, and in the case of jasmine pearls, the additional scent that has been added, ready to be released when unfurled in your cup. This is perhaps why some people believe gunpowder tea is so named less for the shape and more for the explosion of flavor and aroma when it is brewed.

Jasmine pearls

Loosely rolled tea

Gunpowder tea

RUSSIAN CARAVAN AND LAPSANG SOUCHONG

Lapsang souchong is a Chinese black tea with a distinctive pungent, smoky taste and aroma, created by the leaves being smoke-dried over pine wood. Russian caravan tea is also known for its malty, smoky flavors and dark, copper-colored liquid, but is composed of a blend of teas, typically Keemun, Yunnan and other Chinese teas. These teas are not smoke-dried like lapsang souchong, but traditionally picked up campsite aromas while being transported by the tea caravans traveling trade routes across Russia from China (see page 60). The campsite fire and animal smells would have plenty of time to be absorbed by the tea leaves as the journey would take at least 6 months to complete.

More recently, it has become common to find lapsang souchong in a Russian caravan tea blend as a way of enhancing its smoky flavors or for the Keemun or Yunnan teas to be enhanced by smoky flavors before being blended.

ORANGE PEKOE

Most tea companies have a tea called orange pekoe, which has led to the common misunderstanding that it refers to a variety of tea or a tea blend. However, orange pekoe is not a specific tea but rather refers to a grade of leaf, often shortened to "OP" (see page 25). The orange pekoe grade is commonly used for black tea, whether Ceylon, Yunnan or a blend of the two. Tea companies often name any black tea blend that contains some orange pekoe leaves "orange pekoe" and so, confusingly, it has become a common label for any black tea.

TISANES

COMMON TISANE INGREDIENTS

Flowers
Calendula
Chamomile
Jasmine
Rose

Herbs and spices
Clove
Ginger
Mint
Sage

Roots
Chicory
Licorice

Bark
Cinnamon

Fruit
Lemon
Orange
Strawberry

Commonly known as infusions, herbals or fruit teas, tisanes do not actually contain the leaf of the tea plant, but they are often enjoyed in the same way as tea.
A wide variety of herbs, flowers, fruit, roots and barks can be used as ingredients. Before the advent of conventional medicine, tisanes — sometimes referred to as teas — made by blending these natural ingredients were used in many cultures for health and healing purposes. Chinese herbalists in particular claim that almost all ailments and illnesses can be calmed by a natural herbal remedy, sometimes taken in the form of a hot tealike drink. Tisanes are also popular as a naturally caffeine-free way of enjoying a hot beverage.

Lavender

Chamomile

Rose
petals

Mint

ROOIBOS

A bushy plant native to South Africa, rooibos (*Aspalathus linearis*) literally means "red bush" — a rather apt description, as the leaves, which start out a succulent shade of green, turn an earthy red color once processed. They are plucked, oxidized and dried, then infused in hot water — in a similar way to the tea plant. You can also get unoxidized rooibos tea, sometimes referred to as green rooibos, although it is much less common. Rooibos tea has been enjoyed in South African for many years and was first commercially processed in the 18th century. It is naturally caffeine free and goes very well with both milk and sugar, making it a popular, caffeine-free alternative to milky black tea. It is also high in antioxidants so it is often viewed as a healthy tea alternative. Interestingly, it is also makes for a great skin exfoliant when used as a natural face or body scrub.

MATE

Another plant with leaves similar to the tea plant, yerba mate (*Ilex paraguariensis*), is native to South America and enjoyed throughout the continent as an ingredient in a range of beverages from hot teas to fizzy energy drinks. Traditionally, mate is drunk through a *bombilla* (a metal straw with filter) from a gourd (a hollowed-out seedpod bowl), and carried around attached at the hip of the drinker. It is common to re-steep the pale green leaves throughout the day as well as mixing them with other herbs or serving the mate poured over ice. Mate leaves are naturally very stimulating as they contain caffeine, much like tea, and are said to help with concentration, clarity of mind and energy levels.

Mate

Rooibos

Opposite: Popular throughout South America for its qualities as a stimulant, mate is customarily drunk through a metal straw, called a *bombilla*, which has an integral filter to separate the mate infusion from the stems and leaves.

HARVESTING

There are many factors that determine the final quality of your tea, including growing conditions, processing and storage, but perhaps the most fundamental thing to get right is the tea leaf itself. It is important to pick the perfect leaves, with the right method, at the precise time of year, and that the leaves are processed as soon as possible after they are plucked. Harvesting is the job of skilled tea pluckers, often female, whose skills have been passed down through generations.

TEA FARMS AND TEA ESTATES

There are two main types of tea-growing systems, tea farm and tea estate, the latter sometimes called a plantation.

Typically, a tea plantation or estate is a large area under the control of a central organization with multiple fields where crops are grown. This system is common in places like Sri Lanka and India, where many villages were under the central control of colonial tea companies. These companies were set up mostly by the British and quickly bought up most of the land to form large estates that all shared one central factory where processing took place.

There is often a clear hierarchical structure within a plantation, with the plantation manager traditionally housed in a luxurious bungalow on the estate. The workers of the fields and the factory will be employees of the company that runs the plantation and are often housed and fed on the estate, too. Although it is still the case today that plantation owners and managers enjoy very luxurious lifestyles compared to those of the workers, there is less of a "gentlemen's club" mentality on a modern estate.

A tea farm, or a collection of tea farms, tends to be operated by an individual and his or her family, sometimes with help from workers in the local community. The farmer is responsible for all aspects of maintaining his or her fields, as well as growing and harvesting the tea plants. It is unusual for a tea farm to have its own factory or processing facility, so often there will be a community factory shared by a few villages and their farmers, or the farmers will sell their harvested but unprocessed leaves to a nearby company or estate to be processed and sold on. Tea farms and collectives of tea farms are more common in places like Japan, Kenya and some regions of India.

Below: This photograph, taken around 1900 in Sri Lanka (then known as Ceylon), shows workers loading bull carts with cases of tea.

Watched by overseers, tea pickers sort baskets of fresh tea leaves at a plantation established by the British entrepreneur Thomas Lipton in Ceylon (present-day Sri Lanka), circa 1900.

THE LIFE OF AN ESTATE TEA PICKER

In most tea-growing countries it is still very common for the tea estate and factory workforce to be mainly women, but some men are starting to take up the work, too. In most plantations established by the British Empire (for example in India, Sri Lanka and some African plantations) a traditional "womb to tomb" system still exists. These systems and the running of the plantations were heavily influenced by the hierarchical military structure that prevailed in the British Empire during the time of their establishment. The work is hard and the wages still remain low today but the workforce is looked after by the estate from birth until death. The estates provided housing, food and sometimes education for their workforce, and all family members are included in this protection, with new generations also being guaranteed a job for life.

Estate workers in Sri Lanka and India can pick for up to 10 hours a day, 6 days a week and in all weather. They are expected to pick upwards of 35 lb. (16 kg) of tea a day as a minimum but many are pushed to pick over 55 lb. (25 kg). The daily pay is approximately US $2 and tea pickers are expected to work well into their old age.

In recent years some improvements have been made to the lives of estate tea pickers in a large number of countries, including higher wages and better living conditions as well as improved equipment like gloves and backpacks to replace the neck-breaking wicker baskets with carrying straps that went across their foreheads. In countries where education is compulsory for all children, the estate should also ensure that this obligation is fulfilled. However, in some regions it is not uncommon for girls to start in the tea fields from the age of 14 and there is still a long way to go before we can say that significant and consistent improvements have been made across the whole industry.

The introduction of certifications like Rainforest Alliance (see page 68) and Fair Trade (see page 68) has also encouraged estate owners to build relationships with their workers, teaching them about their environment, their jobs and their economy. The certifications also require improvements to be made to buildings and machinery that make life easier for the estate workers. Many estates have seen a decrease in strikes and an increase in productivity as a result of the introduction of these alliances as workforces have higher job satisfaction, easier and safer working environment and a better rapport with the companies for whom they work.

PLUCKING

Harvesting tea leaves by hand is called plucking and is the traditional method of collecting the leaves for processing. Traditionally, tea picking was a female role, as women were considered to be more adept at handling the delicate leaves and men were usually farming or working in the tea factory. Although changes in lifestyle have seen a redistribution of roles, with more women working in the tea factories and some men taking part in plucking, in many countries, such as Sri Lanka, the plucking workforce is still predominantly female.

In order to make most varieties of tea, the pickers will be looking for the top two leaves and the bud of the plant only. The perfect leaves will be light green, still a little curled over and soft, almost downy, to touch. The lower leaves, which are much darker, are too firm and are not suitable for producing the majority of teas.

The method for plucking tea leaves is similar to the motion used to flick a bottle cap from a bottle. If done correctly, this technique will see the shoot pop off into the palm with no need for force or fingernails. Plucking is done with both hands simultaneously and when both palms are full of shoots, the shoots are gently tossed into a basket carried on the back or head.

Once plucked, the bush will grow new shoots within a few weeks and, if the climate is right for producing consistent tea all year round, they will be harvested every 1 to 2 weeks. In areas with a more variable climate, harvests will be done seasonally, one to four times a year.

In areas where tea is harvested all year round, it is common to produce different types of tea during each season's harvest. For example, on many farms in Japan the first spring harvest will be just 1 to 2 days and produces shincha, the most sought-after green tea of the year. Then the late-spring harvest may be for sencha tea, the summer harvest may be for bancha or hojicha, and the last

Left: Using both hands, tea pickers will select and pluck only the top two leaves and the bud of each shoot on a tea bush.

CHA

Cha is the Japanese word for "tea," recognizable in most Japanese types of tea, for example bancha, matcha, sencha, hojicha and genmaicha. The last name literally translates as "brown rice tea."

---

harvest may be for black tea. The farmers will also alter which leaves they pluck from the plant — the finest shoots are best for shincha but, once plucked, they are gone but, come summer, the slightly lower, harder leaves are fine for hojicha. This makes the most sense economically as the skilled tea farmers know how to adapt their methods to ensure that they get the most from their tea plants each year.

At the end of each harvest season the bushes are pruned right back to their brown stalks to encourage new shoots. This makes it easier for the pickers to identify and pluck the best leaves and ensures that the plants stay healthy. It also helps maintain the curved shape of the bush, which again is useful for ease of harvesting: the pluckers can easily walk the paths between the rows and comfortably reach up to pluck at all sides of the bush.

Every 4 to 5 years the plants are put through a "deep prune," when they are stripped right back to their main branches to encourage new growth and renew the plants.

MECHANICAL PICKING

It has become increasingly popular to harvest with the help of machinery in countries such as India, Japan and China and for three main reasons:

1. Accuracy and efficiency of harvesting.
2. Labor is becoming harder to find, as countries undergoing rapid economic growth see workers moving to the cities.
3. Mechanical harvesting is much more cost effective.

The most common tea-harvesting machine is similar to a hedge cutter but has a curved shape and is operated by two people, who walk down the rows of tea, guiding it over the top. The entire tops of the bushes are cut off, branches and all, and air is used to blast the leaves into a bag attached behind the machine.

Compared to mechanical picking, hand-plucking is expensive. In Sri Lanka, for example, labor accounts for

more than 60 percent of the cost of production. A large harvesting machine can harvest a 2.5 acre (1 hectare) field in Sri Lanka in a day — it would take a workforce of between 60 and 90 people to do so in the same amount of time.

There are arguments for and against these machines, with many pointing out that they could never match the quality that comes from hand-selecting each shoot. In most areas where harvesting is carried out all year round and there is a readily available, affordable workforce it has so far made sense to continue to handpick. However, in places like China there is a reliance on technology to automate as much of the process as possible so that small farming communities can afford to produce tea in small teams.

The main concerns are that machines cannot be selective enough and that there is damage to the leaves during the process. For the majority of average-grade tea, this isn't really a concern as the leaves will get sorted, cleaned and cut (by further machines) during processing anyway, so it may make sense to introduce machines, especially during peak harvesting season.

For some higher-grade, specialty teas, such as White Silver Needle (Bai Hao Ying Zhen), there is currently no machinery advanced enough to be able to select only the new buds and delicately pluck them from the stem at exactly the right place. For this sort of rare and luxury tea-harvesting, hand-plucking is unlikely to be replaced in the near future.

Above: Automated harvesting, as is done on this plantation in Thailand, is far quicker than plucking by hand, but is not suitable for higher-grade teas that need the delicate touch and experienced eye of the human picker.

Tea pickers in a plantation near Haputale in Sri Lanka carry lightweight modern backpacks that are designed to be safer and more comfortable to use than the traditional wicker baskets, with carrying straps that go across the forehead.

PROCESSING

There are five main stages of tea processing: withering, rolling, drying, grading and cleaning. For some tea types, there is an additional stage — oxidization.

Tea processing was traditionally completed by hand and was very time-consuming and labor intensive. For specialty teas, varying levels of hand-processing may still take place, as it is easy to damage the leaves with machinery and ruin the resulting tea. However, as demand for tea has grown, commercial plantations have developed a streamlined, almost fully mechanized process.

The main purpose of processing is to reduce the level of water in the leaves. Fresh tea leaves contain nearly 70 percent water so, to produce 1 lb. (450 g) of tea, approximately 4 lb. (1.8 kg) of leaves are needed. A combination of the withering, rolling and drying stages gradually reduces the water contained in the tea leaves to just 3 percent.

Different methods are used and machinery is adjusted, depending on which variety of tea is to be produced, and the various methods vastly alter the appearance, aroma and flavor of the final tea. Although the same freshly picked leaf is used to start with, the different processing methods applied will produce totally different varieties of tea. The main varieties of tea produced are white, green, oolong, black and pu'erh teas (see page 57).

When producing black, pu'erh and oolong teas there is an additional purpose of processing: to encourage oxidization, which further develops flavor and aroma compounds. The oxidization stage is added after the rolling stage, which further encourages this by bruising the leaves and breaking down their cell walls (see page 47).

Before we explore tea processing in more detail, it is important to note that, although the tea-processing journey is similar, each factory will have its own variation in timing, temperature, machinery and method at each stage of the journey.

Even more dynamically, most factories will further vary these factors throughout the year, or sometimes from day to day, in order to adjust the processing to the harvest. Many plantation owners would say that controlling these factors is the most skilled role in the entire tea industry and, even in highly mechanized factories, it still takes years of experience to learn how to set up each stage of the process to produce the perfect teas.

Once plucked, the tea leaves are transported by truck to a tea-processing factory. It is important that the leaves are transported as quickly as possible as they begin to wither as soon as they are plucked.

The leaves are weighed as they come into the factory in order to keep track of how much tea is being plucked out in the fields and produced in each batch. The leaves are then moved, either by hand or by conveyor, to the withering room.

Below: In a tea factory in China's Fujian Province, fresh tea leaves are spread out on bamboo trays to wither — the first of a number of stages designed to reduce the moisture content of the leaves.

WITHERING

In the withering room the leaves are spread out along troughs for 8 to 14 hours, usually overnight. During this time 35 percent of moisture is lost, leaving the leaves limp and slightly shriveled, but still green and fairly large in size.

Traditionally, withering took place on the upper floors of the factory, and the best factories were sited on hilltops so that the natural breeze would aid the withering process. This is why many of the original tea factories have so many windows on their upper floors. However, this method can take days and relies heavily on the right weather, so it has mostly been abandoned in favor of newer technology like withering fans.

The leaves lie on top of wire mesh and the withering fans pump air down the troughs. If the evening is cool, sometimes the air is heated a little, to around 175°F (80°C). Controlling air temperature and flow, as well as turning the leaves a few times, is important to ensure an even withering and to prevent mold forming.

The chemical composition of the leaf changes during withering as the loss of moisture and start of oxidization begin to break down molecules and trigger enzyme activity. Levels of chlorophyll begin to reduce while caffeine levels rise and, most importantly, flavor compounds that are responsible for creating a tea's unique aroma and flavor profile develop.

When producing green tea there is no extended withering stage; instead the leaves go straight to the rolling room to be fired (see "Killing the green" box on page 52). During the production of white tea, the leaves are usually laid in the sun for a slower, natural withering.

ROLLING

Once withered, the leaves are transported to the rolling room, either by hand or by being dropped down through chutes onto the rolling machines on the floors below. The most commonly used rolling machines are big, circular rotators that press the leaves between two grooved wooden plates which tear, squeeze and bruise the leaves. The roller machines can process up to 55 lb. (25 kg) at a time and take about 20 minutes.

Rolling serves three purposes:
1. It squeezes out yet more moisture.
2. It breaks down the cells in the leaves to encourage a faster and fuller oxidization, causing aromatic and flavorful "tea juices," or flavor compounds, to develop. Once dried, the rolled leaves will lock in this flavor and aroma, ready to be released later when they unfurl in your cup.
3. It alters the leaves' appearance and size, which can alter strength and also help stabilize and preserve the leaves for transport and storage.

Once the leaves have been rolled, it is necessary to sift out the right size and shape leaves and send larger

Left, above: Fresh tea leaves being moved to the withering room at the Dambatenne Tea Factory in Sri Lanka. Built by Thomas Lipton, the factory employs 2,000 workers.

Left, below: In the withering room, tea leaves are then spread out evenly on wire mesh in troughs approximately 4 to 5 ft. (1.2–1.5 m) wide, where they will be withered for up to 14 hours.

Opposite: After the withering stage, the leaves are transported to the rolling room, where they are squeezed between grooved plates in rolling machines.

ones back through the roller. This is called roll breaking and is sometimes considered to be a separate stage. Roll breaking can happen up to four times, each time with increasing pressure, and each time tea of the right size and shape is sifted out.

Before the invention of the roller machines, this process was done by hand and would involve over 8 hours of either shaking, tossing in baskets or kneading the leaves, with very similar movements to those used to knead and roll bread dough.

Green teas go through an additional drying stage prior to rolling, if rolling is required. Some green teas are not rolled and white teas are never rolled, unless for the purpose of appearance, as is the case, for example, with jasmine dragon pearls which are hand-rolled and hand-tied.

For most commercial production of green tea, the leaves are passed slowly through a rotating heated machine that sits above coals heated to 150°F (65°C). This is termed "first drying," "firing" or "killing the green" and serves to reduce the moisture in the leaf by 20 percent, halting oxidization before the leaves then go onto the rolling machine (see the "Killing the green" box on page 52).

OXIDIZATION

All tea leaves will have gone through a small amount of natural oxidization during the stages that we have already discussed, but for most oolong, black and pu'erh teas further oxidization is required. This stage is sometimes referred to as the fermentation stage.

Once the leaves reach the desired size and shape from the rolling machines they are laid out to oxidize, usually on long cement tables but sometimes on the cool factory floor. The period of oxidization can be from 30 minutes to 5 hours, depending on the desired outcome. Skilled factory workers can tell when the fermentation period is complete by smelling the leaves.

Factories must determine the ideal time of day to process their teas, depending on the local climate. If it is too hot, the leaves could ferment too much and too quickly, ruining the flavor. For example, in the Nuwara Eliya region in Sri Lanka, whose factories specialize in producing light and fragrant teas, tea processing takes place early in the morning to avoid the hottest hours of the day.

After oxidization the leaves look very different from how they started out, being darker in color and smaller in size, as well as having a distinct aroma.

THE STAGES OF TEA PROCESSING

Once tea leaves have been harvested, they are sent to a tea factory
to be processed. The main stages of tea processing are withering, rolling,
oxidization, drying, cleaning and grading. However, not all types of tea
go through all these stages: some teas go through only
one or two stages, whereas others go through all six stages before being packed into
aluminum-lined paper sacks, ready for shipping — it all depends on the
desired appearance, aroma and flavor of the tea being produced.

1 WITHERING

The leaves are moved to a withering room, where they are placed on wire-mesh racks in troughs. Fans then pump air down through the troughs. The temperature of the air and rate of flow are monitored and controlled to ensure even withering. The leaves are also turned a few times, to stop any mold appearing as they are dried.

White tea is usually laid out in the sun to dry and does not pass through any further processing stages.

FRESH LEAVES

Freshly picked tea leaves are transported — speedily, as they begin to wither the moment they are plucked — to the factory where they are first weighed.

KILLING THE GREEN

After withering, green and oolong teas undergo a first drying stage. "Killing the green," also called "fixing the green," is the heating process that deactivates enzymes in tea leaves to halt oxidization.

A number of different drying methods can be used at this stage, from roasting and pan-firing to steaming the leaves or baking them in an oven.

2 ROLLING

The leaves are then moved to the rolling room, where they are pressed in rolling machines. This squeezes out further moisture and breaks down the cells in the leaves.

Before the introduction of roller machines, tea factory workers had to shake or toss the leaves in baskets for many hours, or knead them by hand.

HAND-ROLLING

Some teas are still rolled by hand today, but less as a method to reduce their moisture content than for reasons of flavor and aesthetics — high-grade green and oolong teas are carefully rolled into neat little pearls.

3 OXIDIZATION

The leaves are now laid out on a table or on the floor to oxidize, an enzymatic process that affects the tea's flavor and aroma, as well as its appearance.

Black teas are fully oxidized but the process is halted earlier when producing oolong teas, which are thus only partially oxidized. The degree of oxidization varies depending on the desired result.

Green and white teas do not undergo this oxidization stage.

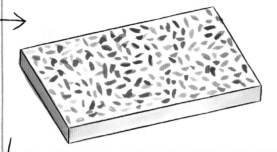

4 DRYING

In order to halt the oxidation process and further reduce the moisture content, the leaves are then dried using conveyor dryers or ovens. Once it has been dried, the tea is shelf-stable — the flavors will stay as they are until the tea is brewed.

For green teas, which have already undergone the "killing the green" process, this marks a second drying stage, and some even go on to a third drying stage.

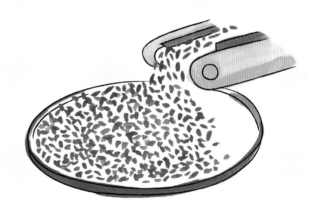

WET PILING

In the past, pu'erh teas would ferment on the long journey from China via the Tea Horse Road. These days, pu'erh teas undergo a much faster ripening process, similar to composting.

PRESSING AND AGING

After drying, pu'erh teas are pressed into cakes or bricks and left to age in a cool, damp place.

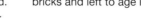

POLISHING (GREEN TEAS ONLY)

Just before packing, some green teas are polished in polishing drums for a couple of hours. This gives the leaves a silvery sheen — a look that is preferred in some markets — but does not change the taste.

5 CLEANING

Stalks, fibers and veins are removed from the dried leaves during the cleaning process. These waste products are often later used as compost.

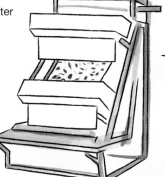

6 GRADING

The cleaned tea leaves then move on to be graded. Grading machines contain layers of mesh of increasing size and vibrate, allowing the leaves to separate according to their size.

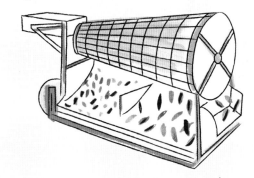

7 PACKING

In the packing room the tea leaves are packed into sacks lined with aluminum. These are then stamped with the tea's grade, weight, package date and origin.

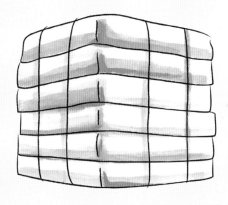

The science behind oxidization

The oxidization process is an enzymatic reaction that changes the chemical structure of the leaf and the tea's flavor, aroma and appearance.

Once the tea leaf is plucked from its stalk, it can no longer be nourished by the normal chemical reactions that take place in the tea plant, so it will begin to break down stored carbohydrates and proteins. When rolled, the surface cells break, releasing enzymes (polyphenols) that absorb oxygen and produce flavor and aroma compounds: theaflavins and thearubigins (see page 20).

"KILLING THE GREEN"

The Mandarin word *shaqing*, which means "killing the green," is the process of heating and deactivating the enzymes in the leaf to halt oxidization. Applied mainly to green and oolong teas, this first drying stage, or "fixing," usually involves turning the leaves by hand in a pan or a wok, baking them in a dryer or passing the leaves through a rolling drum, where they are steamed.

In Japan, a steaming process is used in which the leaves are quickly heated to a temperature of 300°F (150°C) to "fix" the tea. The leaves remain bright green in color and fresh and vegetal in flavor.

In China, tea is usually "fixed" by pan-firing, a process that is slower to reach top temperature. The leaves have a toasty, roasted aroma and are more yellow.

These help create a clean and crisp taste as well as adding body to the tea liquor and turning the leaf darker in color. Heating will deactivate the oxidative enzymes, stopping the oxidization process and preserving the new flavor and aroma compounds.

DRYING

The final drying stage is used to halt the withering or oxidizing of the leaf and to preserve it in a shelf-stable form until it reaches your cup. Some drying methods, such as smoking, can also be used to add flavor to the leaves whereas others can be used to halt oxidation earlier in the process (see the "Killing the green" box below).

There are a variety of drying methods, specific to country and region, each altering the aroma, appearance and flavor of the leaf and the final cup of tea. The most common are oven or conveyor drying, roasting or pan-firing, steaming, smoking and natural drying using the sun or airflow.

The most common drying method for black teas is to pass the leaves through a commercial oven on a slow-moving conveyor. The ovens are heated to 190°F to 235°F (88°C–113°C) and the leaves travel slowly down through shelves, or sometimes in a circular motion, reducing moisture by a further 30 percent. The chemical processes going on in the leaf have now been halted and the moisture level is around 3 percent. The tea leaves will now remain as they are until brewed in your cup.

For green teas, this is a second drying stage and the leaves may also go on to a further, third and final, drying stage. This can be overnight in cylindrical machines similar to cement mixers. These gently turn the leaves over, causing them to curl up.

Most white teas are dried without the use of ovens or fires; they are just laid out to dry naturally in the warm air, often on bamboo mats. This maintains the delicate balance of flavor and nutrients in white tea leaves.

It may be desirable to create a smoked flavor or aroma

Above, left: A worker in a tea factory in India pours tea leaves into the drum of a drying machine.

Opposite, above: White teas are dried naturally by laying the leaves out on bamboo mats in the open air, as is done here at a tea garden in Fuding in China's Fujian Province.

Opposite, below: Workers in Assam, which is both India's and the world's largest tea-producing region, load a commercial tea dryer with leaves.

during tea production, for example to produce a tea like lapsang souchong. This type of smoked drying was originally achieved by accident along the trade routes of the Russian caravans (see page 32). The modern method of creating these types of flavors still involves fire and wood, but usually in the form of pine wood being added to a commercial oven through which the tea is passed.

CLEANING AND GRADING

Once dried, the leaves pass through to a separate, cooler room in the factory to be cleaned, sorted and graded.

Cleaning consists of removing stalks, fibers and veins from the dried leaves to ensure that the quality of the batch is at its highest. Most cleaning machines use static to attract the stalks and fibers, filtering them out from the desirable leaves. More advanced cleaning machines use color cameras and sensors to detect the light-brown color of the stems and shoot blasts of air to blow them down a different chute to the tea leaves.

Grading is the process of separating out different sizes of leaf into batches. Most grading machines are rotary shifters, made from layers of mesh sieves of increasing size, that vibrate to filter out the leaves according to particle size.

Depending on the factory, there might be 6 to 20 grades of tea separated out at this point. Some factories specialize in producing a certain grade of tea but most will look at the current market to determine the most desirable tea at that time and adjust their process to suit. They may also use a tea-cutting machine to cut larger leaves into small pieces should they wish to produce broken grades or CTC to suit market demands (see page 25).

The waste products of tea production — the light-brown fibers and stalks — are often gathered and recycled in the form of compost. In some cases, they are cut and processed as cheap, low-quality tea, deemed suitable for consumption by the local market.

Opposite: Green tea is still dried by hand in some places in China. It is pan-fired by tossing it in a large wok over an open fire.

Right, above: Most cleaning is done by machine, but in some regions it is still done by hand. At this tea factory in Mae Salong in Thailand, women carefully sift through the leaves, removing stalks, fibers and veins.

Right, below: Tea passes through a grading machine into bags at a tea factory in Tamil Nadu in India. India is the world's second largest tea producer, after China.

BANANAS AND APPLES

Comparing the tea process to what happens to a banana or an apple makes it easier to understand.

If plucked from the plant and left, the banana or apple will turn brown on its own over time — this is like the withering stage.

If heated and dried, much like banana chips or slices of apples in a pie, the fruit will not turn brown but be preserved in its natural color — this is like the drying or fixing stage.

If you leave a banana in your bag all day, it will begin to turn brown where its surface has been bruised and so starts reacting with the oxygen in the air — this is like the rolling and cutting stage.

Left: Having passed through all the processing stages, the tea is packed and labeled, ready for shipping to customers around the world.

PACKING

Finally, the tea leaves are packed into aluminum-lined paper sacks in the packing room and stamped with their grade, weight, packed date and factory/estate origin. In cooperatives or in countries where the tea industry is centrally owned, operated or regulated, there is usually a set weight that each grade of tea must hit for a full sack.

In the packing room of a green-tea factory you might also see a machine that polishes the leaves for 2 to 3 hours, to an almost silvery shine. There is no specific reason why some green teas are in higher demand in a polished form, as it doesn't alter the taste or aroma of the tea at all.

UMAMI

A high-quality batch of matcha should have no hint of bitterness and fantastic umami. Along with the more familiar sweet, sour, bitter and salty, umami is one of the five basic tastes, commonly used in Japan to describe a distinctive savory note found in foods containing a specific amino acid — glutamate. Meat broths and foods that have been fermented or aged are usually high in umami, and the taste is also associated with an intensive mouthfeel. Other foods that are said to be rich in umami components include mackerel, seaweed, yeast-based spreads like Marmite, shiitake mushrooms, parmesan cheese, soy sauce and green tea — in particular matcha.

MATCHA TEA PRODUCTION

Matcha is powdered Japanese green tea and it is enjoyed as part of the spiritual tea ceremony as well as in everyday life. Matcha has become increasingly popular all over the world in recent years thanks to its health benefits. Because you are consuming the whole of the leaf, ground up, you benefit from a very high level of antioxidants, vitamins and minerals — much higher than you would get by infusing green tea leaves in hot water as is customary.

Most Japanese matcha is grown in the Uji region of Japan, near to the ancient capital Kyoto. The tea plants used for matcha are shaded 2 to 6 weeks before harvest, traditionally by topping them with straw or building a bamboo shelter around them; today black sheets are used. This technique stops sunlight getting to the leaves and slows the final period of growth. This does two things to the plants — it causes an increase in the levels of chlorophyll and amino acids in the leaves and encourages very tender, fresh shoots to emerge. This will ensure that the leaves, when plucked and processed, are bright green, full of flavor and moisture and with no hint of bitterness.

Once harvested — the highest-quality matcha is plucked by hand — the leaves are sorted, cleaned and partially dried before being refrigerated. In this state the leaves are called *tencha*. As the leaves that are perfect for producing matcha can be harvested only once or twice a year, it is important that they are refrigerated within the subsequent 48 hours, which allows the *tencha* to be used to make matcha all year round.

To produce matcha, the *tencha* leaves are dried again, to remove all but 3 percent of the moisture. Then, traditionally, they were ground on a handcarved millstone. Using this traditional method takes around 1 hour to slowly grind 1 oz. (30 g) of matcha powder. The grinding process cannot be completed any faster, as speeding it up would create too much friction and heat the matcha powder, as well as making it impossible to produce the finest of powder.

Modern matcha factories have mechanical grinders that can grind a much larger quantity of *tencha*. The grinding rooms of a matcha factory are always in darkness and temperature controlled to ensure that the bright green color and flavor are not damaged during processing.

PROCESSING SPECIFIC TEA TYPES

WHITE TEA

The process for white tea is very simple, involving just the drying stage. The leaves are handled very delicately and allowed to dry naturally in the open air or tumbled on a very low heat in a drum, if the region has damp or cold weather. There is no oxidization or rolling stage, unless the leaves are being formed into pearls or flowering tea. This gentle process produces a light, furry leaf or bud and a delicate flavor once the tea is brewed.

GREEN TEA

Green-tea processing is common in Japan and China, including Taiwan. There is usually an additional drying stage for green teas, sometimes called "Killing the green" or "fixing," where the leaves are heated to pause the oxidization process, usually by pan-firing or steaming, before being rolled and shaped (see page 52). Pan-firing involves turning the leaves on large, heated metal drums. For the steaming method, the leaves are passed through the steam chamber for only 30 to 120 seconds. The drying method used at this early stage will add interesting aromas and flavors to the green tea, with pan-firing often imparting roasted notes and steaming bringing out grassy and oceanic flavors. The leaves will then later go through the final drying stage to make sure that they are fully dry.

OOLONG TEA

Oolong goes through all of the processing stages but is only partially oxidized. The process of oxidization is similar to black tea but the leaves are left for a shorter time before drying. They are also rolled and shaped, sometimes multiple times, before drying. They tend to share some of their characteristics with both green and black teas, being more complex in taste than green tea but not as strong as black teas. There is a huge range of oolongs, with oxidization anywhere between 5 and 80 percent, and rolling taking a wide variety of forms.

BLACK TEA

Black teas are nearly always produced on a large scale using automated machinery and go through all of the processing stages. Black teas can either be whole leaf or cut up to expose more of the surface area of the leaf to the oxidization process — this creates the strong black tea taste enjoyed with milk by most Western tea drinkers.

PU'ERH TEA

Pu'erh teas also go through all of the processing stages, including oxidization, but are then packed into cakes or bricks and stored in a dark, humid place over a long period of time before being sold. This is sometimes referred to as fermenting but it is more like an aging process that creates a complex, earthy and malty taste. Some pu'erh teas are aged over many years, much like a whiskey or a wine.

Sencha green tea

Matcha tea

Pai Mu Tan white tea

White Silver Needle tea

A shaded tea field in Japan. Shading tea for a few weeks before it is harvested increases the chlorophyll levels in the leaves, turning them deep green and making them rich in flavor. High-quality Japanese teas — gyokuro as well as tencha — used for matcha are shade-grown in this way.

A SHORT HISTORY

Our humble beverage, tea, has such a rich and dramatic history that started nearly 7,000 years ago in the remote monasteries of China. From its early history, when tea played a fundamental part in health, spirituality and custom, it was traded in the furthest corners of the world along some of the most dangerous and intrepid trade routes known to humanity. Wars have been fought over it, kings have been dethroned because of it, whole nations have depended upon it. A lot has happened over the years to bring your daily cup to your table. More recent trends have seen a real surge in tea drinking, especially of specialty, herbal and blended teas.

THE DISCOVERY OF TEA

There are a multitude of stories surrounding the first discovery of tea, with perhaps the most famous of them being the story of the mythical Emperor Shennong, who enjoyed drinking a cup of boiled water in his garden every day. One day, while he was sleeping, a few leaves from a nearby *Camellia sinensis* tree dropped unnoticed into his pot of water while it was boiling, thus creating the first cup of tea. Shennong, who is said to have been born in the 28th century BCE, is also credited with inventing the plough and teaching the people of China how to farm the land.

Whether this fable is rooted in reality we cannot say, but the oldest official discovery of cultivated tea plants dates to around 6000 BCE, on the remote Tianluo Hill in eastern China. Tea was originally cultivated in monastery gardens and prescribed as a medicinal tonic to relieve a variety of conditions including vomiting and fatigue, as well as to elevate the spirit or improve the constitution. It remained both a spiritual and medicinal beverage until much later during the Tang Dynasty (sixth to ninth centuries CE) when the first book about tea was written by Lu Yu, a writer from Tianmen. In *The Classic of Tea*, Lu Yu relates the myths surrounding the origins of tea in China and describes how tea is grown, harvested, processed, brewed and consumed.

During this time tea grew in popularity for its taste as much as for its medicinal reputation, but it was still produced on a fairly small scale and remained largely reserved for the spiritual and the elite. The ceremony of serving and storing tea was becoming an increasingly important part of demonstrating wealth and culture for the ruling classes in China and so foreign visitors were regularly served tea in welcome.

It was around this time that tea was introduced to Japan by Buddhist monks who brought back tea seeds from study visits to the monasteries of China. Again, tea was shared between the monasteries and the ruling class and went on to play a central part in both ceremony and spirituality in Japan.

SPREADING ACROSS ASIA

During the 12th century, the Japanese Zen monk Eisai became fascinated by the Chinese approach to tea. He wrote a book titled *Kissa Yojoki* (*How to Stay Healthy Drinking Tea*), in which he described the benefits of tea for both health and spirituality and likened it to the Zen Buddhist principles of balance and harmony. Eisai introduced the warrior class, the Samurai, to these principles as well as to the Chinese fashion of the time for

Above: Legend has it that Emperor Shennong accidentally discovered tea in 2737 BCE when leaves from a wild tea bush dropped into his cup of water.

powdered tea and this soon spread in popularity among those seeking spiritual balance.

In the 15th century the tea ceremony as we know it today was set out under the leadership of the Zen Buddhist Sen no Rikyu and today the art of tea ceremony is still taught by his descendants. By the 18th century an exciting period of tea innovation occurred, with new methods for producing tea, such as the Uji method (see page 212), being developed in Japan. Another influential discovery was that canopy shading helped develop the mellow, sweet notes and highest grades of gyokuro and matcha. This boosted the popularity of these types of tea both in Japan and abroad.

EUROPE AND BEYOND

The French, British and Dutch were all trading with the Far East during the 17th and 18th centuries and soon became aware of the ancient tea industries of China and Japan. The trade routes that passed over Russia by land and around Indonesia by sea enabled European merchants to spread tea all over the globe. In many European countries tea was adopted by the wealthy upper classes as both a luxurious treat and a way of demonstrating their wealth.

Tea became particularly popular in Britain where it was enjoyed in all manner of situations and led to the invention of new concepts such as tea gardens, where people would stroll around beautifully manicured gardens and socialize over a cup of tea. Another great social invention of this time was afternoon tea (see page 29). In 1839, Britain ended up going to war with China following disagreements around the illegal trade of opium and so its tea supply was threatened. The British had already noticed that another, very similar, strain of the tea plant was growing wild in the northern regions of India and set about cultivating their own tea plantations there.

It is highly likely that the commercial tea industry would have been established regardless of the challenges the British faced with trade in the Far East during this time, but war with China certainly acted as a catalyst. The cultivation methods used by the British in India paved the way for a new strain of the tea plant, *Camellia sinensis* var. *assamica*, that would enable cultivation of tea in many more countries. During the 19th century tea plantations were set up in India and Sri Lanka by the British, in Indonesia by the Dutch and in Vietnam by the French. Turkey and Iran also started cultivating tea, the former under Ottoman rule and the latter under the individual efforts of the Iranian prince, Mohammad Mirza.

In the 20th century Kenya, Thailand and Argentina started to develop their own tea industries and all three countries have quickly made their mark on the international tea stage.

HOW TEA IS TRADED TODAY

The main stages of tea trade are as follows:
1 Growing
2 Trade with a factory for processing (unless the tea is grown on a centrally owned estate and factory)
3 Blending
4 Trade with a broker
5 Trade with a packaging company (in some countries, brokers do the blending and packaging before selling the tea on)
6 Trade with a wholesaler
7 Trade with a retailer
8 Sale to the end consumer.

It is not unusual for there to be three or four levels of trading to wholesalers and retailers, who then sell the tea on to others. Tea is also traded as a commodity investment.

The international tea trade has a few major players, some of whom are also producers and some of whom are not. Unilever and Tata, for example, are involved in all stages of trade, from owning estates in producing countries to running brokerages that buy and trade the tea, as well as distribution and blending houses that then go on to distribute it, all under their own brand. For the majority of the other players in the market, there is a large chain of trading that takes place, sending the tea on its journey across the world. Some tea changes hands tens of times before you pick it up in your local supermarket.

Although there are some international bodies that report on the tea trade around the world, such as the Food and Agriculture Organization of the United Nations, there is no global regulator for the trading of tea. Some countries, such as Sri Lanka, have a centralized government-run body that regulates the trade of tea, both in terms of setting prices and restricting those wanting to become brokers, but many others have no such organization.

Left: Tea clippers sit alongside sailing ships in London's East India Docks in 1892. Designed for speed, clippers were used to transport tea to Europe quickly to supply the growing demand for this new commodity.

Opposite: A small group enjoys a tea party below blossoming cherry trees in this woodcut print by the Japanese artist Kitao Shigemasa (1739–1820).

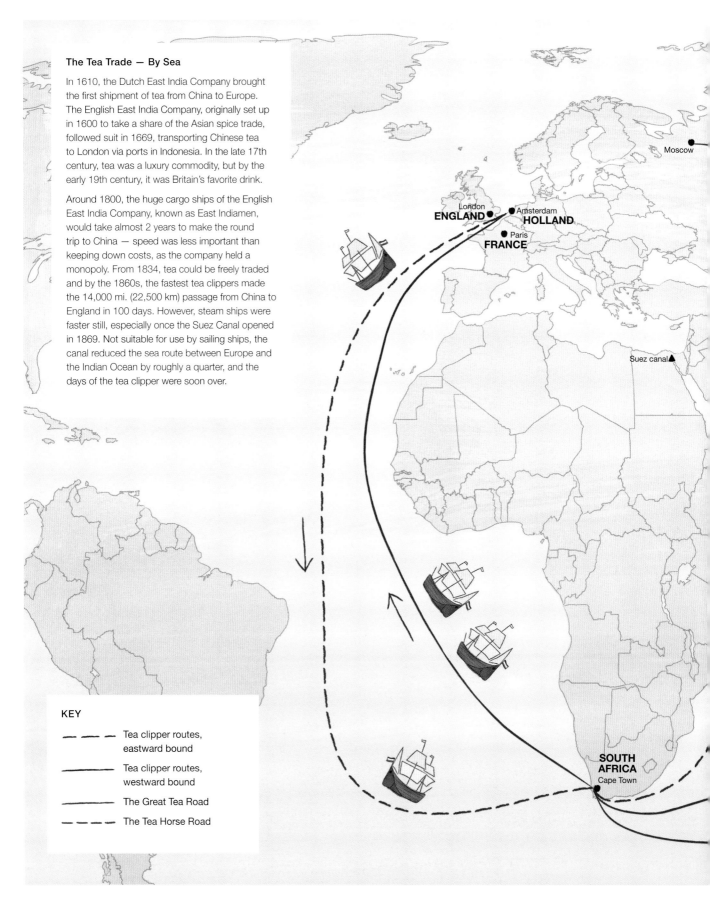

The Tea Trade — By Sea

In 1610, the Dutch East India Company brought the first shipment of tea from China to Europe. The English East India Company, originally set up in 1600 to take a share of the Asian spice trade, followed suit in 1669, transporting Chinese tea to London via ports in Indonesia. In the late 17th century, tea was a luxury commodity, but by the early 19th century, it was Britain's favorite drink.

Around 1800, the huge cargo ships of the English East India Company, known as East Indiamen, would take almost 2 years to make the round trip to China — speed was less important than keeping down costs, as the company held a monopoly. From 1834, tea could be freely traded and by the 1860s, the fastest tea clippers made the 14,000 mi. (22,500 km) passage from China to England in 100 days. However, steam ships were faster still, especially once the Suez Canal opened in 1869. Not suitable for use by sailing ships, the canal reduced the sea route between Europe and the Indian Ocean by roughly a quarter, and the days of the tea clipper were soon over.

Moscow

London
ENGLAND
Amsterdam
HOLLAND
Paris
FRANCE

Suez canal

SOUTH
AFRICA
Cape Town

KEY

— — — Tea clipper routes, eastward bound

———— Tea clipper routes, westward bound

———— The Great Tea Road

— — — The Tea Horse Road

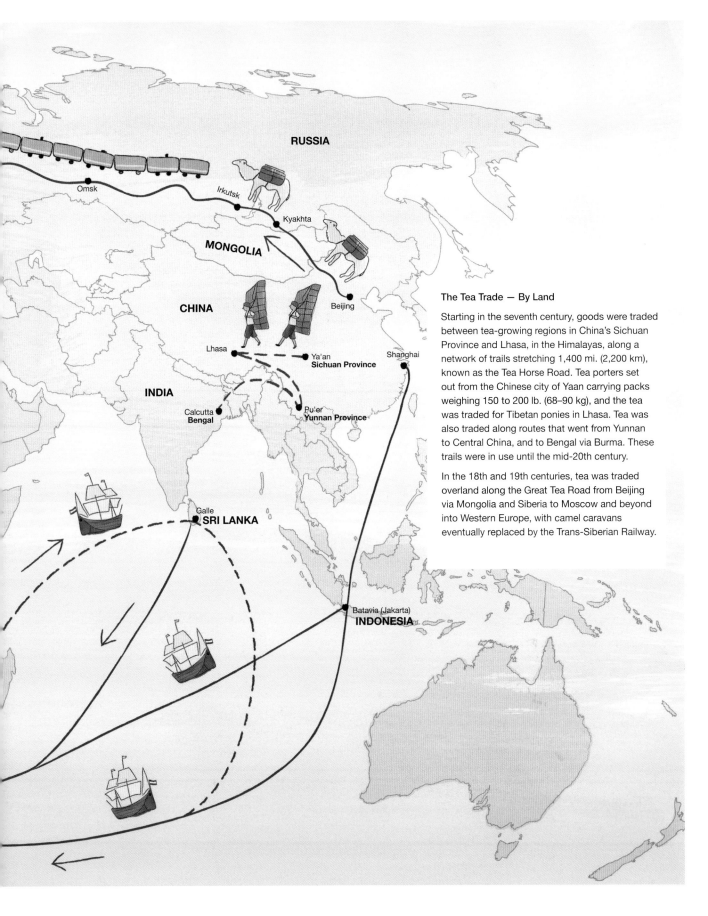

RUSSIA

Omsk

Irkutsk

Kyakhta

MONGOLIA

CHINA

Beijing

Lhasa

Ya'an
Sichuan Province

Shanghai

INDIA

Calcutta
Bengal

Pu'er
Yunnan Province

Galle
SRI LANKA

Batavia (Jakarta)
INDONESIA

The Tea Trade — By Land

Starting in the seventh century, goods were traded between tea-growing regions in China's Sichuan Province and Lhasa, in the Himalayas, along a network of trails stretching 1,400 mi. (2,200 km), known as the Tea Horse Road. Tea porters set out from the Chinese city of Yaan carrying packs weighing 150 to 200 lb. (68–90 kg), and the tea was traded for Tibetan ponies in Lhasa. Tea was also traded along routes that went from Yunnan to Central China, and to Bengal via Burma. These trails were in use until the mid-20th century.

In the 18th and 19th centuries, tea was traded overland along the Great Tea Road from Beijing via Mongolia and Siberia to Moscow and beyond into Western Europe, with camel caravans eventually replaced by the Trans-Siberian Railway.

THE QUESTION OF SUSTAINABILITY

Although not a necessity, tea is certainly considered a daily commodity by millions of people across the world. The production, trade and consumption of this little beverage has a huge impact on society and the economy on both national and global levels. Yet its future is threatened. Unfortunately, some of the best regions for producing tea are those most vulnerable to challenges such as climate change, political instability, disease and population growth. These factors, plus shifts in food-buying culture toward more cost- and convenience-led products, are damaging the industry dramatically, so sustainability needs to be an absolute priority.

THE ECONOMIC AND SOCIAL IMPACT OF TEA

Tea is grown in 35 countries and traded in many more, providing jobs for many millions. Think of all the people involved in the long journey from plant to cup: plantation workers, tea pickers, estate pruners and gardeners, factory processors, leaf rollers, leaf graders, brokers, traders, blenders, wholesalers, retailers and tea drinkers.

It is easy to see how negative changes to the tea industry can have a ripple effect that has much more devastating consequences than just not being able to get our daily fix of tea. On a micro level, it is common for a tea factory or estate to be the backbone of an entire village's economy, often in some of the poorest parts of the world. On a macro level, tea can be one of a nation's leading exports, supporting the whole economy.

For the tea industry to continue to support all these people and economies, there must be positive changes to sustainability across many areas, encompassing everything from the workforce — people's livelihoods, communities and skills — to the plantations — production methods — and to our planet — protecting the land and climates needed to grow tea, as well as the market economy.

CHALLENGE 1: CLIMATE

Tea production relies on a steady supply of water and energy, both of which could become less readily available over the coming years in some parts of the world. As well as this, the ideal regions for growing tea are also those that are the most vulnerable to changes in temperature and rainfall due to the effects of climate change. This change can affect all agriculture, so not only does tea production suffer directly, the tea industry is also likely to be battling against staple food crops for access to fertile land and resources.

Already in India and Sri Lanka, increased temperatures and rainfall have had an impact on the dry and wet seasons that naturally regulate tea production. An increase in rainfall can lead to soil erosion while the higher temperatures cause increased periods of drought, as well as encouraging a wider variety of pests and diseases that can attack the tea plants.

CHALLENGE 2: POPULATION

Dramatic population growth in many tea-producing countries has seen an increase in demand for tea, which is good. However, increased population means increased urbanization so land previously used for tea production is in demand for housing and other crop production.

The increase in demand for tea also means many producing countries are starting to consume their own teas, rather than exporting. Combined with emerging economies, such as those of the Middle East and Africa, joining the tea market, this creates even more demand and puts pressure on supply. Another factor to consider is that tea plucking and processing is hard manual labor and currently pays little. As the population grows, more people are moving to cities to take up better opportunities, which creates a shortage of labor in the tea plantations and factories. This further encourages mechanization of the tea-production process, and although this can aid efficiency of production, it also means that those training up to enter the tea industry are few and far between.

LOW-INCOME FOOD-DEFICIT COUNTRIES

The Low-Income Food-Deficit Countries (LIFDC) is a list, collated by the Food and Agriculture Organization of the United Nations, of the world's poorest nations as determined by income and basic food-stuff deficits. A country finds itself on the LIFDC if its citizens fall below an acceptable income or basic food-stuff level, as set by the United Nations and the World Bank.

Of the 54 countries on the list in 2015, 20 of them produce tea and 33 export tea. That means that a significant 60 percent of the poorest countries in the world rely on tea as part of their fragile economies. Even more remarkable is that two of the world's top five tea-producing countries — Kenya and India — are on that list, while a third country, Sri Lanka, only graduated from it in 2015. Once on the list, a country can only be removed once it has constantly risen above the deficits for three consecutive years.

The LIFDC highlights some key facts for the tea industry: 2,383,121 tons (2,161,931 tonnes) of tea each year is produced in countries where the workforce live in poverty, are malnourished and earn low wages. It is obvious that the tea industry has the potential to have an important impact, both positive and negative, on the livelihood of millions of people currently living below the poverty line.

CONSUMER RESPONSIBILITY

As the culture of food choice, especially in the Western world, is becoming more price- and convenience-led, consumers are becoming less and less connected with the origins of the foods they eat. It is not unusual to buy food with little knowledge about where it has come from, the costs of its production or even its ingredients or its potential impact on our health.

It is great that tea is loved enough to be considered an everyday commodity but this leads to a presumption that tea is, and always will be, readily available and cheap to buy. While mainstream tea companies battle each other to offer the lowest prices on the supermarket shelves, the whole supply chain is having to match these pressurized demands. This leaves the industry open to poor-quality tea being produced and workers being treated, and paid, unfairly in order to achieve the lowest price for the tea.

For the tea industry to be preserved for the people who work in it and for the environments needed to produce good-quality teas to be sustainable, there is a level of responsibility on you, the tea consumer, to consider where, how and at what cost the tea in your cup is produced. Paying a little more for good-quality teas that you know have been sourced ethically, that support the communities that work to produce them and that taste excellent, too, has a much healthier end result.

PARTNERSHIPS AND CERTIFICATIONS

With all of the above in mind, there are various schemes, organizations, partnerships and certifications that have been established with the aim of changing the tea industry for the better.

Fairtrade

The Fairtrade initiative has an honorable aim: to ensure that companies pay a fair price for products so that producers and farmers are able to support themselves. The way it works is that all Fairtrade products are sold at a preset price that is determined (by Fairtrade) after examining all market factors. In 2015 this was between US $1 to $1.50 per kilogram of tea, depending on the country.

The benefits are obvious: because the farmers are guaranteed this price, they are able to afford to invest in their children, their business and their community. Fairtrade also does a great deal to support and educate independent farmers in tea-producing regions.

However, the common misunderstanding that Fairtrade means free trade can be damaging. The main problem is that control and decision-making are still not in the hands of the producers and the current system of tea buying, trading and selling is always going to make the end trader the most money and the producer the least — the value is added at the final branding and selling point. Therefore, it could be better to address the system as a whole and link up the producers with the end sellers at a more balanced level, rather than simply adding a few extra pennies onto the price of tea.

Rainforest Alliance

Rainforest Alliance focuses on educating and supporting tea producers to produce tea without impacting negatively on the surrounding wildlife. They teach and assess sustainable farming methods, offer staff training and education, and monitor levels of pesticides and soil erosion.

It is to the benefit of everyone, especially the farmer, to look after tea farms for future cultivation, but it is expensive to become Rainforest Alliance certified. This can often mean that only the larger plantations and corporations become certified, adding a premium to the price of their product at market and negatively impacting on those who cannot afford it.

Ethical Tea Partnership

The Ethical Tea Partnership (ETP) combines a bit of what both Fairtrade and Rainforest Alliance do. Again, it strives to make improvements to the tea industry by monitoring and certifying producers and sellers that meet preset standards, providing support and education for the producers and also helping combat climate change through the tea industry.

The ETP works by charging a joining fee to tea sellers and retailers who want to become members of the partnership. To be approved, they must be able to prove they buy tea from sources that are deemed ethical when judged on a wide variety of conditions set by the ETP. These include the health and safety of the workforce, sustainable growing practices and other similar standards. The ETP then uses the money raised through membership and other charitable donations to give back to local tea communities, setting up workshops and placements to educate and raise standards.

Opposite: A tea picker at Chamraj Tea Estate. Located in the Nilgiri Hills of Tamil Nadu in South India, the estate produces ethical tea and has both Fairtrade and Rainforest Alliance certification.

PART TWO

TEA BREWING AND DRINKING

TEA-BREWING BASICS

There are a few key elements to consider when preparing the perfect cup of tea, including water quality and temperature, how much tea to use and brewing time. Although making a cup of tea may seem a relatively simple task, making small adjustments to technique and equipment could greatly improve the flavor and quality of the end result. These tips on key elements and basic brewing techniques will help with your day-to-day tea preparation and the more advanced brewing techniques will allow budding tea connoisseurs to really come to grips with how to make the most of different varieties of tea.

THE KEY ELEMENTS

WATER

Water is just water, right? Not necessarily. As a cup of tea is 99 percent water, the quality and taste of the water you use will affect your final cup of tea. Oxygen in the water plays a crucial role in infusing the tea leaves, drawing out their flavor and releasing their aroma. The mineral content of water can also impact on the infusion process and resulting quality.

It is best to use freshly drawn cold water but be wary if you live in an area where your tap water is "hard" or has an unusually high level of chlorine, fluoride or lime. If this is the case, you may want to consider filtering it first or using bottled spring water.

It is also important to refill your kettle with fresh water each time you boil it. If you fill your kettle with water from the hot tap or use water that has been previously boiled you will have a "flat" cup of tea, or one with scum floating on the top. This is because the water contains less oxygen, which is needed to allow all the tea flavors to properly infuse in your cup.

LOOSE LEAF VERSUS TEABAGS

There is a long-standing debate on the use of loose-leaf tea over teabags, with the main argument for loose leaf being its higher quality and the main argument against it being convenience. Since their (accidental!) invention by the American Thomas Sullivan in the early 1900s (see the box on page 74), teabags have been seen as the "fast-food" cousin to loose-leaf tea and, in the past, rightly so, as the quality was indeed significantly lower.

Originally, Sullivan's silk pouch teabag wasn't readily adopted outside of the United States for this reason, but after the invention of the rectangular paper teabag with tag and string in the 1950s, the lower-quality tea found in teabags was forgiven, or perhaps forgotten, by consumers as the teabag rapidly became a commodity.

In recent years the quality of some teabags has improved dramatically, as has the choice on offer — even on the supermarket shelf. Key players in the tea industry have successfully educated the everyday shopper in what to look for, and what to expect from their teabags and the desire for higher quality "whole-leaf teabags" has grown. Teabags are no longer seen as just a value or commodity item and consumers are more than happy to spend more on their tea to ensure higher quality and taste.

Left: Hop pickers relax with a cup of tea after a day's work in the hop fields in Kent, England, in 1932.

WHO INVENTED THE TEABAG?

In the early 1900s New York tea merchant Thomas Sullivan began sending out his loose-leaf tea samples in fine silk bags. The popular infusers (see page 85) in this era were metal balls of a similar size and shape to Sullivan's silk bags so it is believed that some customers mistook the bag itself for an infuser and placed it directly into their teapots.

Obviously, the tea didn't infuse very well through the silk but Sullivan saw this as the start of a great invention, so adapted the bags, making them from a mesh gauze material, with a string and tag. These early teabags became quite popular in the United States over the next few decades.

It was in 1950s Britain, during the era of convenience gadgets and time-saving inventions, that the teabag took off outside of the United States. The ease of using the teabag over the teapot won over the hearts and mugs of an entire nation and then spread across the world.

Today teabags are very much an essential on any grocery shopping list, with over 95 percent of the tea market being teabag users.

No matter how convenient the teabag may be, many people still love taking the time to visit a specialty tea shop to choose their favorite loose leaves and getting out the teapot on special occasions.

TEMPERATURE

Water temperature is also an important factor in developing the taste of tea: too hot and the tea will taste bitter, too cool and the tea won't be able to infuse to its full potential.

In most circumstances freshly boiled water is fine, but to get the absolutely perfect water temperature for each tea type, you should aim for 204 to 208°F (96–98°C) for black teas and around 176 to 185°F (80–85°C) for white teas, greens and oolongs. All types of tisanes, including rooibos and mate, can take boiling water without the taste being affected.

There is a general misconception that lighter teas, such as green and white teas, have a bitter, tannin taste.

When brewed correctly, this should not be the case. To put it simply, the bitterness is due to the water temperature being too high and burning the leaves. To go into more detail, different flavor compounds dissolve at different temperatures, with many of the sweeter and more aromatic flavors being caused by amino acids that dissolve around 140°F (60°C) and most of the bitter, astringent flavors being caused by tannins, that dissolve around 176°F (80°C). The key to a perfectly balanced cup of green tea is to get just the right amount of each compound dissolved without letting any one of them overpower the others.

It is possible to be even more technical about various leaf types and even time of harvest in determining the optimum brewing temperature (again, this is down to the level of amino acids and other compounds found in the leaves) but as a general rule follow the brewing temperature chart on page 77.

HOW MUCH TEA?

For most teas, use a heaped teaspoon per 12 fl. oz. (350 ml) of water (this is the capacity of the average tea mug). Some people like to follow the tradition of adding an extra spoonful "for the pot" when using a teapot. You can do this if you prefer a very strong flavor or if you are using particularly large mugs or cups.

With some teas — oolongs, for example — you can re-steep multiple times, leaving the leaves in the pot or infuser to use again. Rinse the leaves in cool water once you have removed them, then place on a plate or saucer to reuse at a later point in the day.

STRENGTH

Everyone has their own ideal strength of tea, often determined by its color once brewed. However, strength can be used to describe not only a measure of color or flavor intensity but also the depth of flavor.

Using a larger amount of tea, increasing the temperature of the water and altering the brewing time can all impact on the strength of a cup of tea. If you take your tea with milk, it is important that you use enough tea and that you leave it long enough to infuse so that the addition of milk doesn't drown out the flavor.

Opposite: Making up over 95 percent of the tea market, teabags were invented by the New York tea merchant Thomas Sullivan in the early 20th century.

BREWING TIME

If you are using everyday teabags, brewing time isn't so much of a concern, as they are designed to be infused quickly. The tea leaf particles inside a teabag are small, so the increased surface area makes them perfect for quick "dunking." If you are using a whole-leaf teabag or loose-leaf tea the brewing time should be adjusted accordingly.

Whites, greens and oolongs shouldn't be left for more than 3 minutes. This is for the same reason as making sure the water temperature isn't too high (see above) — to ensure the tea doesn't taste bitter.

Black and pu'erh teas should be left for 3 to 5 minutes, with a longer brewing time if you are taking your tea with milk. Some black teas can develop a strong tannin taste if you over-steep them, so be careful.

Herbal, rooibos, fruit and mate teas can be left for as long as you like as they do not contain the polyphenols that make the tea leaf turn bitter when over-brewed. These tea types should be brewed for at least 4 minutes, but you can leave them longer if you like a stronger flavor.

MILK, SUGAR AND LEMON

It was the British who started the tradition of adding both milk and sugar to tea in the late 1700s. Until then, all types of tea were enjoyed without, with one exception: some farming communities in the mountainous regions of northern Asia would add animal butter or milk to their tea as a way of consuming more calories to keep warm, as well as adding salt to help with hydration (see page 162).

Whether this influenced the British habit of drinking tea with milk is unknown, but other possible explanations include the belief that adding milk to the cup before the hot tea would protect fine china from cracking and staining, or the belief that taking milk with tea would benefit health. The British also enjoy some black teas with a very thin slice of lemon, which is allowed to infuse into the tea but removed before drinking. These additions seemed to be a uniquely British custom, as few of their neighbors adopted taking tea with milk or lemon.

Adding sugar to tea isn't quite so uniquely British, as people in many areas of eastern Europe and Russia like to enjoy very sweet black teas. It is thought that the addition of sugar in Britain was originally a way of masking the bitterness and low quality of some tea, particularly during World War II, when tea was scarcely available and rationed. A much more recent development, American iced tea is also highly sweetened (see page 117).

Adding milk or sweetener is a personal preference but with some tea types, such as green, white and most oolongs, this will ruin the flavor and should be avoided.

Opposite: A mobile canteen supplies Indian soldiers with tea outside a mosque in Woking, England, during World War II.

BREWING CHART

TEA	TEMPERATURE	BREWING TIME	ADDING MILK
White tea	176°F (80°C)	3 minutes	No milk
Green tea	176°F (80°C)	3 minutes	No milk
Oolong tea	176–194°F (80–90°C)	3 minutes	No milk*
Black tea	194–207°F (90–97°C)	3+ minutes**	With or without milk
Mate	207–212°F (97–100°C)	4+ minutes	No milk
Rooibos	207–212°F (97–100°C)	4+ minutes	With or without milk
Herbal	207–212°F (97–100°C)	4+ minutes	No milk
Fruit	207–212°F (97–100°C)	4+ minutes	No milk

* Most oolong teas should be treated like green tea, so taken without milk, but some are nearer to a light black tea so could take a small amount of milk. Milk oolong is especially flavorful with a dash of milk.

** Always leave black tea to brew for longer if you are adding milk.

Tea drinking as a social activity is epitomized in this photograph of "Gibson Girls." In the early 20th century in the United States so-called Gibson Girls, named after the illustrator Charles Dana Gibson, strove for an idealized form of beauty, fashion and etiquette.

MISS CARLYL

MISS CLARKE „THE GIBSON GIRLS.

TEA TOOLS

Most tea lovers take pleasure in the ceremony of preparing their favorite tea with their preferred collection of tea utensils and tools. Tea tools play an influential role in tea culture in many societies, not only because of their impact on the resulting flavor but also because of their symbolism and beauty. The most common and best-loved tool for brewing tea is the teapot but infuser baskets or balls are also commonly used. Innovative new gadgets, which make it easier to prepare loose-leaf tea, have helped fuel a revival of convenience-led tea preparation that doesn't sacrifice flavor.

CHOOSING THE RIGHT TEAPOT

The use of a bowl-like vessel in which to brew tea leaves dates back thousands of years in China, but spans nearly all tea-drinking cultures. Traditionally, the bowl-like teapot would hold and infuse the leaves in hot water and, when ready, the tea would be poured through a small hole, mesh or strainer into a cup. This ensured that the leaves remained in the pot and only the freshly brewed tea ended up in the cup. The modern-day teapot design with handle, lid, spout and sometimes built-in infuser basket or mesh strainer was invented only in the 16th century.

In many cultures a teapot plays a unique part in tea ceremonies and other social occasions, not only in preparing perfect-tasting tea, but also in conveying ceremonial messages through its use and even its design. Many teapots are elegantly hand-painted, and using an intricately decorated teapot has long been a sign of class and sophistication in the Far East, and later in Europe, too.

When choosing a teapot, it is important to consider whether you want something functional or eye-catching, as well considering the right size for your needs. You will also need to think about whether you will be brewing loose-leaf tea in the pot, or using teabags. If it is the former, you will also need either an inbuilt infuser basket or a strainer to pour the tea through (see page 85).

There are thousands of designs of teapot available, with the option of matching your teapot to your kitchen décor or even to the season. The teapot used in a Japanese tea ceremony, for example, is chosen to reflect the time of year or occasion. Along with the other items of tea ware used in the ceremony, the teapot can feature designs that reflect the changing seasons, from cherry blossom to falling leaves.

Teapots can be made from a variety of materials, such as unglazed stoneware, porcelain, glass, cast iron, silver and stainless steel — all of which affect the taste of the resulting tea in unique ways. Some materials are better suited to certain varieties of tea.

Below: The silver tea service takes pride of place in *The Tea* (*c*.1880), a painting by the American artist Mary Cassatt (1844–1926), who lived and worked in Paris in the late 19th century.

A mid-19th-century Qing Dynasty Yixing teapot mounted with pewter and jade-mounted lid, spout and handle.

A Qing Dynasty Yixing teapot (c.1820) by Yang Pengnian (1767–1831) with calligraphy by Chen Mansheng (1768–1822).

A Chinese porcelain teapot (1890) with floral decoration.

CLAY

Teapots made from pottery materials such as clay have been hand-fired for tens of thousands of years, originally in China. As a general rule, the higher the firing temperature, the harder the resulting ceramic. Clay is a popular material for teapots, as they tend to retain heat very well. Glazed or unglazed finishes are possible.

The first "official" teapot is the Yixing clay teapot, which dates back to 16th-century China. Yixing ware was made from porous clay and left unglazed so that the pot would absorb the aroma and flavors of the tea it contained. A clay teapot is therefore great for enhancing stronger flavors from roasted Chinese greens, malty pu'erhs and smoked black teas. But, because of the absorbent nature of the clay, it is important that you have a different pot for each type of tea.

For the same reason, if you are using an unglazed ceramic teapot, you must also ensure that you never wash it out with soap, as it will retain the taste of the soap — instead, just rinse it with cool water, ensuring that all leaves and particles are removed, and then leave to dry. This is perhaps where the long-standing belief that you shouldn't use soapy water to clean any teapot, let alone put it in the dishwasher, comes from. However, many modern porcelain teapots designed for everyday use are dishwasher safe, and washing them with soapy water will not affect the taste of the tea.

PORCELAIN

True porcelain, a type of fine, translucent white ceramic fired at a high temperatures, originates from China, where it was refined during the 13th and 14th centuries. It is made of ground china stone mixed with kaolin, also known as china clay. First developed in Staffordshire, England, around 1800, bone china is a type of porcelain made by adding a bone ash to the china clay and china stone mixture. Bone china is often very similar in appearance to true porcelain, but there are subtle differences, mainly in weight, translucency and thickness.

Porcelain teapots are great for lighter teas such as greens, oolongs and lighter black teas such as Darjeeling. Bone china is often considered to be the finest teapot material and, despite its premium price tag, its delicate and elegant appearance makes it the top choice as part of an afternoon tea set.

A clear-glass teapot with central glass infuser, based on a design by the German industrial designer Wilhelm Wagenfeld (1900–90).

This style of teapot is a familiar sight in modern homes.

A Japanese Edo Period (1603–1868) cast-iron tea kettle, or *tetsubin*, decorated with hailstone motif.

GLASS

It could be said that glass is an impractical material for a teapot as it doesn't retain heat awfully well, it stains easily and is fragile. However, glass teapots are perfect when brewing beautiful teas, especially flowering teas, as they offer a mesmerizing view of the leaves infusing in the pot. They also allow you to see when your tea has reached the perfect strength. It is common for a glass teapot to come with a matching warmer, which allows you to place a candle under your teapot to keep it warm.

CAST IRON

Cast-iron teapots originated in Japan in the 17th century, where they are known as *tetsubin*. Cast iron had been being used prior to this point to manufacture vessels in which to heat water on top of a fire, as the iron heats up quickly and retains heat well once at the desired temperature. Its more specific use for loose-leaf tea dates to around the same time that loose-leaf sencha tea (as opposed to powdered matcha tea) became popular in Japan. A teapot made out of cast iron is similar to one made of unglazed clay in that it absorbs some of the flavors of the tea it contains. It is therefore likewise important that you do not use soap to clean a cast-iron teapot. You should also dry it thoroughly after use, to prevent it rusting.

Often decorated with intricate patterns, cast-iron teapots rapidly became a status symbol in Japan and were often given as luxurious gifts. They remain to this day the most expensive teapots to own but their skilled, handmade manufacture means they can last a lifetime.

BREWING THE PERFECT CUP OF TEA

1. Fill the kettle with freshly drawn cold water from the tap, or spring water, if desired.

2. Once it has boiled, pour a little water into the teapot and swirl around to warm the teapot slightly, then pour the water away. This is to ensure that the pot will retain as much heat as possible.

3. Add to the pot the required number of heaped teaspoons of loose-leaf tea or teabags for the number of cups of tea you are making.

4. Fill the pot to the desired level with the correct-temperature water, trying to cover all of the tea leaves as you pour. Water straight from the kettle will be 207 to 208°F (97–98°C). If you require a water of a lower temperature for optimum brewing, you can either use a temperature-controlled kettle or add one-fifth cold water to the pot before the boiled water and use a thermometer to gauge the temperature accurately.

5. If there are some leaves floating on the top of the water, stir with a teaspoon to coat them with water.

6. Replace the teapot lid and leave the tea to brew for the desired time (see the brewing chart on page 77).

7. Once brewed, if you are using a simple teapot (without a built-in infuser) pour the tea through a strainer into the cup. If you are using a teapot with a built-in infuser, remove this before pouring out the tea.

8. Add milk, if desired, and enjoy. If you are not taking milk, allow the tea to cool slightly before drinking.

INFUSERS

If you are just starting out with loose-leaf tea, the most cost-effective tool is a decent in-cup infuser. These come in all shapes and sizes, but all work by providing a mesh barrier between the leaves and the hot water in the cup. Once your tea is brewed, you simply remove the infuser and are left with a perfectly infused cup of tea.

Loose-leaf tea drinking has enjoyed a revival in recent years and many innovative tools and gadgets have been invented to make it hassle free, such as an infuser basket that clips onto the side of your cup, allowing you to drink your tea while it is still attached. This lets you test the strength of the tea, to ensure the perfect infusion time, before removing the infuser. Alternatively, you can leave it in place: many people who drink herbal teas prefer not to remove the leaves at all while they drink their tea.

Another cheap way of brewing loose-leaf tea is to use disposable paper sacs. You add a spoonful of your chosen tea leaves to the sac, creating your own DIY teabag. Some sacs have a drawstring, like a teabag, while others are a tall, rectangular shape, with the top of the sac designed to sit over the edge of the cup. The former are better, as they are more easily moved around the cup to encourage infusion and they do not drip.

Another option is to use a tea strainer which differs from an infuser as it is held over or balanced on the cup and tea is poured through it from the teapot into the cup. The strainer catches the leaves as the tea goes through it. Strainers look a bit like oversized spoons, are usually made from stainless steel and can be ornately designed.

INFUSER MUGS AND VACUUM FLASKS

Tea infuser mugs, where the infuser basket is built into the design, are becoming increasingly popular. These can be great for making just one cup, when you don't want to bother with a teapot and strainer. Infuser mugs are made up of a mug with fitted infuser basket, that sits in the mug on a lip just below the top, and a lid that fits neatly on top. The infuser basket works just like any other infuser but the handy addition of the lid helps keep the water hot while brewing and then converts into a saucer to hold your dripping infuser basket, once removed. Infuser mugs are a fairly modern invention but are really practical to use in places like the office or at school where you may not have access to a teapot.

Another recent innovative invention to hit the tea market is a vacuum flask with inbuilt infuser. For many years vacuum flasks have been used to transport either premade tea or hot water but a loose-leaf vacuum flask allows you to prepare and transport tea in just one device and will keep your tea steaming hot for several hours. You can also leave your tea leaves to brew while you are on the go.

Ball infuser   Collapsible basket infuser   Clip-on infuser

A wide array of clay teapots with different glazes and finishes on display at a busy market in Kowloon, Hong Kong. The first clay teapots were hand-fired in China tens of thousands of years ago.

GRAVITY STEEPERS

The gravity steeper is a fairly modern invention that is set to take loose-leaf tea drinking to a new level. Its design is similar to that of a teapot in that it holds hot water and tea leaves, and it can be used to brew and pour tea. However, the gravity steeper differs from a teapot by having a fine mesh over the bottom of its brewing chamber that acts as a strainer when the tea is poured. The really clever part is the way the brewed tea is poured into your cup — you simply place the gravity steeper on top of the teacup, which causes a gatelike mechanism to open and the tea to drain through the mesh, leaving the leaves behind in the chamber and the tea in your cup.

Once you lift the gravity steeper up off your cup, it automatically stops pouring so there is no dripping or mess. You can then simply empty the tea leaves into the garbage (or add them to your compost heap) and give the steeper a rinse. The whole thing comes apart for easy cleaning and it can also go into the dishwasher.

HOW TO BREW USING A GRAVITY STEEPER

1. Add tea leaves to the gravity steeper.

2. Fill with freshly boiled water and leave to brew for the desired time (see page 77).

3. Place the gravity steeper on top of the tea mug.

LOOSE-LEAF KETTLES

At the premium end of tea-brewing equipment are electric kettles that not only heat water to specific temperatures but also brew the leaves for you. Temperature kettles have been around for a while, and are great for setting the correct water temperature for specific types of tea. Loose-leaf kettles are a much more recent invention and take tea brewing one step further by letting you set the temperature and also the brewing time.

The kettle works by heating water in a glass chamber to the desired temperature, which is set by you, and then a built-in leaf chamber is lowered into the water for the desired period of time, again set by you. Once the tea is brewed, the leaf chamber is lifted out of the water and you can pour the tea just as you would water from a normal kettle.

These kettles are great for precise brewing but, just like any other specialized tool, they require attention and effort to keep them clean and serviced. Also, although it is possible to brew up to five cups of tea at a time, it requires all five tea drinkers to be drinking the same tea type, so if you want to prepare different types of tea, a standard kettle and individual infuser baskets might be a better option.

COMMERCIAL TEA TOOLS

For coffee-shop owners, the type of coffee machine they use is probably the top consideration and the equipment often takes center stage in the shop. Commercial tea tools aren't quite so glamorous or essential: many tea rooms require only a good urn and a selection of teapots or infuser baskets. Just as with brewing at home, it is important to consider the water quality, temperature and brewing time, so a decent teashop or café would always have a good-quality water filter fitted to its urn and use timers and thermometers for optimum results.

Over the last few years, a few commercial tea machines have been invented that are slowly being tested out across the globe. These machines ensure absolute precision, speed up service and allow more elaborate tea-based drinks, such as tea lattes, bubble tea and iced teas, to be made. Manufacturers are also developing machines that take single-serving pods of tea, like the capsule coffee machines that are popular for use at home.

Above: Cafés and tea shops use urns or boiling-water taps for speed and convenience when making pots of tea.

BUYING AND STORING TEA

You can buy tea in a wide variety of places, ranging from supermarkets to specialized tea merchants, so there is plenty of choice. But buying the right tea for you doesn't need to be confusing. The keys are to first establish your own preferred tastes, find a knowledgeable tea supplier that you trust, be prepared to try something new and to store your tea correctly once you get it home. Unless you sample it first, there is often no way of guaranteeing you will like a tea when you purchase it for the first time. Here, however, we will explore a few ways of improving your odds.

SUPERMARKET, TEA MERCHANT OR ONLINE?

Do have a look in your local supermarket, especially when initially figuring out your tastes, as there is often a good-quality brand or two available. Be aware, however, that it is not necessarily the case that if, for instance, you like a certain brand's English breakfast teabags you will also like its loose-leaf sencha. This is because a lot of supermarket tea brands specialize in everyday grocery-type teas, which are consistent but low grade. It is also worth noting that beautiful packaging does not guarantee high-quality tea.

Most prepackaged teas sitting on a supermarket shelf should list information about strength, tasting notes and brewing methods to help you decide before you buy. This information can also be found on the product pages of online stores. It's also a good idea to look at online reviews from other tea lovers, as this can help you get a true feel for how the tea tastes.

In order to try the higher-quality, more specialized varieties of tea you will need to visit a decent food market, the food hall of a high-end department store or a specialized tea merchant, either in person or online. A good tea merchant will often have the most choice and in-depth knowledge to be able to guide you to something you will like. Sometimes it is also possible to try samples but make sure that you ask how the sample has been prepared, checking whether they have added any sugar, for example. A tea merchant should be able to answer any questions that you have about harvest, origin, freshness, traceability and flavor notes. If they can't, then you might want to try somewhere else.

GRADE AND QUALITY

You should be able to examine the dry leaf, whether in store or online, and this will help you determine ingredients and quality. Fuller, brighter leaves that are a consistent color are usually a strong indicator of high quality. If you prefer smaller leaf grades, you want to make sure that the particles are all consistently the same size and that they do not contain any twigs or stalks — a telltale brown color often gives these away.

Below: This 1930s poster from the Empire Marketing Board, formed in 1926 to promote trade throughout the British Empire, urges consumers to buy Ceylon tea and Canadian salmon.

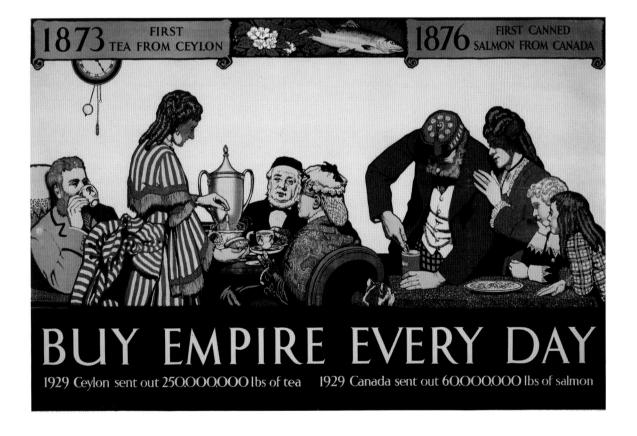

Siwa - Thee schmeckt gut

ORIGIN AND FRESHNESS

One of the best things to ask the staff at a specialized tea store is whether they have a direct link back to a grower or estate. If they do not, it is likely they are buying from a catalogue of teas held by a tea-blending house or broker (see page 62). This can sometimes mean the tea isn't as fresh, as it often sits with the broker for a long time before reaching its end retailers. It could also be an indication that the proprietor or tea company isn't as knowledgeable about their products as you would hope.

HOW MUCH TO BUY

Most tea merchants sell by weight and, as a general rule of thumb, it is often best to start out with the smallest quantity and to try a few varieties to figure out what you might like. If you discover the taste for a particularly specialized or expensive tea type, it is still best to buy in smaller quantities, more regularly, so that it is fresher. However, if you are purchasing a tea that is only harvested once a year, you may want to invest in a larger quantity to last you all year. As with any tea, it is important that you then store it correctly when you get it home.

Opposite: A Japanese woman wearing traditional costume enjoys a cup of tea in this German advertising poster. Siwa was an Anglo-German tea-importing business.

Right: Jars of tea for sale in Dashilar Street. Located near Tiananmen Square, this is Beijing's oldest and most famous shopping street.

STORING TEA AT HOME

1. **KEEP IT AIRTIGHT.** It is important to keep your tea in an airtight container to prevent it going stale. Most tea is sold in airtight packaging of some variety, such as a plastic pouch or an airtight tin, but not all packaging is resealable. If you can't reseal the original packaging, you will need to transfer the tea into an airtight caddie or tin that seals well.

2. **STORE IT IN A DARK PLACE.** Tea is sensitive to light and, if left in sunlight, it will lose flavor so, although glass jars look pretty, they are not suitable — tin or plastic containers are better.

3. **KEEP IT COOL.** Tea is affected by heat as well as light. A cool place like a cupboard should do fine for storage. There is no need to refrigerate tea.

4. **KEEP IT DRY.** An airtight tin in a cool cupboard should also keep tea nice and dry, which is perfect, as damp tea goes moldy.

5. **KEEP IT AWAY FROM STRONG SMELLS.** Tea is incredibly sensitive to aroma so keep it away from any strong smells, such as cooking food or cigarette smoke, and always replace the lid and put away the tea as soon as you have finished with it.

The busy packaging hall of an English tea-trading company in 1932. As we can see here, this was work carried out mainly by women.

TEA TASTING

We drink tea in a wide variety of everyday situations and circumstances: socially with friends, during meetings or appointments and as part of our daily routine. But have you ever paused for a moment to consider what your tea really tastes like? What the leaves look like or what scents fill your nose as you sip? This is what tea tasters and brokers do every working day: putting your cup of tea through rigorous tasting tests, to ensure the correct balance of aroma and flavor. If you pause not just to drink, but truly to "taste" your teas, you will be sure to discover a sensual world of flavor and enjoyment.

PROFESSIONAL TEA TASTING

Being a professional tea taster might sound like the perfect job: getting to sip tea all day long. In reality, it takes years of experience, an in-depth knowledge of the tea-growing process, excellent sensory perception and a brilliant set of taste buds.

Tea tasting occurs at various stages on tea's journey to your cup. At the plantation each harvest will be tasted for grading and quality; at larger tea-buying markets wholesalers will be tasting as they look for teas to export, and tea companies will send their tea tasters to find the perfect cup to sell on to their customers.

For the tea companies, in-house tasters are also responsible for tasting every batch to make sure that each cup sold is consistent. This is a complex and skilled job as tasters must be able to detect the most subtle of differences between almost identical varieties and grades of leaf. It is crucial that all the elements of the tea-tasting process are precise and identical each time, including the

---

Below: Professional tea tasters inspect the wet leaves as well as tasting and sniffing the tea liquor.

THE PROFESSIONAL TEA TASTER'S TOOLS

Ceramic cupping set
Spoon
Scales
Freshly filtered water
Timer
Tasting wheel/note card (see below)

tea weight, the water quality, temperature and volume, the equipment and technique, and the brewing time.

THE "SLURPING" TECHNIQUE

A "cupping set" is used for tasting tea and is always white in color to allow examination of both the liquor and the leaf. The set consists of a small cup with a lid, in which the tea leaves are placed along with the water to brew, and a small, rounded cup from which to taste the tea.

Once brewed, the wet leaves are left to be examined on the lid of the cup while the tea liquor is observed, then

sniffed and then "slurped." An effective "tea slurping" technique aims to spray the tea over all the tongue's taste receptors while the taster inhales air to elevate the flavors. It may seem like bad table manners, but the louder the slurp the better. Once tasted, the liquor is spat out rather than swallowed.

One can either slurp straight from the cup, as a professional would, or use a spoon to slurp from.

For professional tasting, the tea is prepared a lot stronger than it is intended to be enjoyed at home, by using more tea leaves and a longer steeping time. This is to allow the complex flavors and aroma to develop to their maximum potential.

TASTING PROFILES

During a tasting session the leaf appearance, both dry and wet, the aroma of the leaf and the liquor, the mouthfeel and the flavor will all be examined. The tea leaves are graded and tasting notes are developed, using standard vocabulary to describe the tea.

Some of the standard descriptions include:

Body — with a full strength
Bright — bright-colored liquor
Brisk — lively and invigorating
Coppery — in color, not taste
Deep — can refer to both color and depth of flavor
Dull — the opposite of bright
Flat — lacking in full flavor; no body
Floral — flowery notes
Malty — hoppy notes, rich and deep
Mellow — even, full taste with no bitterness
Pungent — astringent but not bitter
Rounded — smooth, complete taste
Tannin — astringent taste often described as bitter
Thin — not much body or strength
Tippy — white or golden tips are present
Vegetal — vegetable notes; fresh and earthy.

Tasting notes will often go even further than these more general terms, often with the help of a tasting wheel that attributes both positive and negative flavors and aromas to the tea. Each tea variety has a different flavor profile on the tasting wheel so a flavor that is positive for one variety of tea may be negative when detected in another.

For example, when tasting a milk oolong, a "nutty, butter" taste profile may be a favorable, positive flavor; however, if tasting a lapsang souchong, this would be a negative flavor or aroma as you would be looking for a positive "smoky, wood" profile, and vice versa.

Opposite, above: Darjeeling, a light high-country Ceylon or an English breakfast blend would go well with the cakes and sandwiches served at a traditional afternoon tea.

Left: A tasting wheel is a useful tool when assessing the flavors of tea.

TEA AND FOOD PAIRINGS

Tea is a great partner for lots of foods and can create an interesting discussion at a dinner party or tasting club. Similar to wine tasting and pairing, different teas go well with different food types, as some will contrast with, and others complement, certain flavors and aromas.

If you want to try your own tea and food pairings, take a look at the suggestions below as a starting point, but remember that most of the fun is finding your own preferred pairings!

FOOD	TEA
Gelato or ice cream	Earl Grey or lavender-scented black tea
Fried foods	Strong, malty teas such as Assam, lapsang souchong or Kenyan black teas
Spiced foods	Complement with a strong tea as for fried foods or contrast with a floral jasmine green tea
Chocolate	A low-country Ceylon, Darjeeling or any hibiscus-based fruit tea
Smoked cheese	Genmaicha, Chinese roasted green teas or apple fruit teas
Salmon	Darjeeling, Earl Grey or a light oolong
Afternoon tea	Darjeeling, light high-country Ceylon or English breakfast blend

THE HEALTH BENEFITS OF TEA

Tea has played a big part in supporting people's health and well-being in many cultures across the world for thousands of years. Its rich history as a medicinal remedy starts in China where, rather than being enjoyed primarily for its taste, tea was prescribed for all sorts of ailments such as fatigue, headaches and even consumption (tuberculosis). In more recent years, people have been turning to herbal teas in an effort to avoid caffeine but the health benefits of tea are not limited to the herbal sphere. Significant research has been completed on the benefits of green, black and white teas, particularly around the positive effects of their antioxidant levels. Being more than 95 percent water, tea can also help you stay hydrated, which boosts both mental and physical functions.

THE RESEARCH AND EVIDENCE

As we have already discussed, tea contains antioxidants and minerals such as magnesium, zinc and potassium (see page 20). Antioxidants can have a positive effect on health by working to combat free radicals that can cause damage to the cells in the body. Consuming high levels of antioxidants has been proven to help lower the risk of heart disease, stroke and some cancers.

Tea is also a good source of fluoride, which is helpful for healthy teeth and gums. Although drinking a very large amount of black tea can stain your teeth, the fluoride will help to strengthen them, too, and reduce bacteria in your mouth.

Numerous studies have also been conducted to test long-standing beliefs that tea can lower cholesterol, aid digestion and slow aging processes, particularly of the skin. Many of these findings are still being developed, so that more can be learned about tea's effects on the body.

CAFFEINE

Following the coffee boom of recent years, there have been concerns about the negative effects of caffeine, a natural component of both coffee and tea (see page 21). Caffeine is completely safe if consumed in reasonable quantities. In fact, it can cause positive side effects such as energy boosts and more alert cognitive function. The recommended maximum dose of caffeine is 400 mg a day — equivalent to four cups of coffee, three energy drinks or 10 cups of tea.

It is interesting to consider the effect of caffeine in tea specifically when compared to coffee. As we discussed earlier (see page 20), some of the natural compounds found in tea — polyphenols such as catechins, antioxidants and the amino acid L-theanine — affect the absorption rate and effects of caffeine on the body. The physical side effects

such as a racing heart or shaking limbs are much less dramatic, but increased energy levels can be prolonged.

It is important to note that different types of tea contain different levels of caffeine. As a general rule, more processed teas contain higher levels of caffeine, as it tends to develop during the prolonged withering and fermentation stages (see pages 46–47). White tea (see page 57) usually has the least amount of caffeine because it does not undergo these lengthy processes, though this is not always the case. This is because some white teas are made from the very youngest shoots and buds of the plant, which often have a high level of caffeine in their cells as this helps to repel insects and other predators that like to munch on the nutritious young leaves.

> ### DOES GREEN TEA CONTAIN ALL THE GOOD STUFF?
>
> Geen tea has a reputation for being healthy because of its reduced caffeine and increased antioxidant content. The absence of an oxidization stage during the processing and the additional drying stage (see page 52) mean that the tea leaves retain a lot of their original chemical structure, retaining antioxidants and not developing as many caffeine compounds.

Below: The maximum amount of caffeine we should consume daily is 400 mg, which is equal to four cups of coffee, three cans of energy drink or 10 cups of tea.

PART THREE

TEA BLENDING

TEA BLENDING

The main aim of commercial tea blending is to create the perfect taste, appearance and aroma for each buyer and then to ensure that this blend is consistently produced all year round for many years to come. Blending tea at home is a relatively easy task, and it can be very rewarding to develop a blend you really enjoy.

There are three main reasons for tea blending:

1 Commercial tea blending is a way of ensuring consistency of batch on a mass scale.
2 Blending tea leaves with herbs and spices for the purpose of holistic health has a rich history in both Chinese and Indian cultures.
3 Blending, scenting or flavoring teas is a popular way of adding interesting and more complex flavor notes to your favorite teas.

COMMERCIAL TEA BLENDING

An essential part of the tea industry, tea blending goes hand in hand with tea tasting — both are usually the responsibility of specialists at tea brokerages or blending houses.

Batches of tea can vary because of changes in the weather, or because of pests, plucking and processing methods, even when plucked during the same harvest or grown on the same estate. For these reasons, it is usually more stable to blend together a number of teas that have been harvested from a variety of areas and sometimes across a number of harvests. Therefore, tea blending is a very important part of the industry as sellers rely on their tea blenders and brokers to ensure that the teas they buy are always consistent for their customers.

Above: Commercial tea blenders mix teas from a variety of sources to achieve a consistent result for their customers, who expect their favorite cup of tea to taste the same every time.

TEA-BLENDING TECHNIQUES

Creating interesting blends by mixing herbal ingredients with tea is not a modern invention. However, as the modern tea drinker looks for a wider variety of flavors and options from their tea offering, the use of blending herbs are becoming increasingly popular.

There are three main tea-blending techniques: blending herbs, inclusions and scenting. When creating a tea blend you may use one of these techniques or a combination of them to achieve your desired flavor.

1. BLENDING HERBS

The most common blending herbs are rose, chamomile, peppermint, hibiscus, ginger and mint, and they are mixed in various amounts with tea leaves to create a desired tea blend. Typically, ingredients such as roots, spices, fruits and herbs are blended for either taste or medicinal purposes. You can also omit the tea leaf itself to blend a purely herbal, and usually naturally decaffeinated, blend. These are commonly referred to as tisanes or herbal teas.

The blending itself can be done by hand or commercially in big mixing drums, similar to cement mixers. To ensure consistency, the weight and percentage of each ingredient is recorded to ensure that an identical-tasting blend can be made again.

2. INCLUSIONS

Inclusions are ingredients that add an aesthetic or health element to a tea blend but do not alter the taste or aroma. Inclusions are commonly used when focusing on blending for health purposes, when taste and aroma are often secondary factors. That said, inclusions can actually make or break the flavor of a good tea blend and innovative tea blenders use them with skill. Even though they add nothing to the taste profile, they are able to add colorful aesthetics that can "trick" our mind into visualizing the taste that we are about to enjoy.

For example, a strawberry tea blend can be difficult to create without the heavy use of flavorings. However, if you add big chunks of dried strawberries or just carefully selected luscious-red inclusion ingredients, the drinker's mind is already thinking of strawberries even before the tea touches their taste buds.

Goji berries can be added to a tea blend as an inclusion. They will change the aesthetics but not the taste of the resulting tea.

Thin slices of orange can also be used to add color, aroma and texture to a tea blend.

3. SCENTING

Interestingly, tea can adopt distinct aromas from the environment where it is grown. For example, many Japanese teas that are grown near the sea are oceanic and vegetal in flavor once brewed. You can also add scents to tea at either processing or blending stage, depending on the aroma you wish to impart. The most commonly used scents are jasmine, traditionally used to scent delicate white and green teas, and bergamot oil, which is used to scent the more modern Earl Grey blend.

Tea can be scented during processing by using fresh blossoms such as jasmine, orchid or rose. This practice dates back thousands of years and originated in the Chinese province of Fujian. The blossom is laid out on top of the processed, dried leaves for up to 4 hours. This is done during the evening to prevent the blossom from opening too soon. For highly specialized teas the flowers may be changed for fresh ones and the tea put through further scenting rounds to ensure the best-quality aroma. Once this is achieved, the tea is then dried again to ensure that it remains fresh until brewed in your cup.

Aromatic ingredients such as rose petals, jasmine blossom or lavender flowers can also be added in dried form during the blending stage but, unlike with the above scenting method, the petals are left in the final blend.

Using an essential oil such as bergamot is a much newer method of scenting tea. The oil is often applied during blending stage: it is sprayed onto the leaves in batches while they are turned to ensure an even distribution. Most fruit flavors in tea are developed using a combination of blending ingredients and essential oils, which help enhance both the aroma and the taste. There are three main types of flavoring oil used across the tea industry: natural, nature-identical and synthetic.

Natural flavoring refers to a scent, oil or essence that has been taken or manufactured from a natural ingredient, such as an orange or a rose. Nature-identical flavorings have the same molecular make-up as their natural counterparts, but are made in a laboratory. Many teas are flavored with nature-identical flavoring oils as they are cheaper to produce, are more stable than natural oils and aren't limited by seasonal variation. Lastly, synthetic flavorings are those that do not match the molecular make-up of anything found in nature.

TEA BLENDING IN AYURVEDIC MEDICINE

Ayurvedic practice centers on the belief that human beings are made up of, and influenced by, three natural energies, or *doshas* — *vata*, *pitta* and *kapha* — that need to be kept in balance for general well-being and health. Although all these energies are working inside us, the Ayurvedic belief is that one will be more dominant. To keep balanced, we may want to reduce the effects of one energy or increase the levels of another.

One of the main ways to do this is through what we eat and drink. As the tea plant has been growing in India for hundreds of years, it has been blended with Ayurvedic herbs and spices as part of this belief system. Some Ayurvedic tea blends are "tridoshic" (that is, suitable for all types of *dosha*) whereas others aim to balance out a dominant *dosha*.

An example would be a cardamom and lavender blend, which would aim to reduce the anxious, restless effects of *vata*. These healing tea recipes have been passed down through the generations and are still enjoyed by many Indians today.

Dried cornflower petals mixed with tea leaves make a fragrant tea.

A wide variety of colorful dry ingredients for use in tea blending are offered for sale at the Mısır Çarşısı bazaar in Istanbul.

BLENDING TEA AT HOME

Many people choose to create their own tea blends at home because they have specific taste preferences, it is relatively quick and easy to do and usually cheaper than buying blends, and also because the process of trying lots of different combinations until you find the perfect one for you is fun. You can either choose to create a blend purely from ingredients you have purchased or use the herbs and plants you have in your garden. A combination of the two works very nicely, too.

WHERE TO BUY BLENDING INGREDIENTS

Many ingredients that are great for blending can be found in the herb and spice aisle of your local supermarket, whereas other, more specialized ingredients can be found at health-food stores or on the internet, often in small quantities and for a reasonable price.

Spices like cinnamon, cloves, star anise, cardamom and peppercorns work well when you are creating homemade black chai teas, and ingredients like ginger,

coconut (flaked or desiccated), cacao nibs, licorice root and chilli can be combined with many tea types to create really flavorful blends. If you are interested in blending a more subtle tea, stick to floral or fruit ingredients. You should purchase them dried, and herb and spice stores, be they local or online, are again the best places to find these ingredients.

Many ingredients are sold loose and unwrapped, so be sure to transfer them to airtight containers. Any ingredients sold in plastic wrappers should also be kept in airtight containers once opened.

Below: Lavender coco-licious rooibos tea is made with some unusual, and delicious, ingredients. See page 114 for the recipe.

Rooibos tea

Lavender

Cacao nibs

Desiccated coconut

INGREDIENTS YOU CAN FIND IN YOUR GARDEN

The great thing about blending your own teas is that there are plenty of ingredients that you can find in your garden or at your local garden center.

You can either make a "wet" blend (using freshly plucked ingredients from your garden, such as mint leaves or rose petals) or a "dried" blend (using ingredients that have been through a dehydration process, such as dried rose petals or dried mint leaves), depending on your preference, and the time and equipment available to you. Ingredients that are good to add to a wet blend are mint

Lemon and fresh mint

(there are many varieties of mint — pineapple mint and licorice mint are particularly effective), nettle, lemon balm, chamomile, rose, lemon verbena, fennel (leaves or seeds) and coriander (leaves or seeds). You simply pick the fresh leaves, flowers, roots or seeds, crush them between your palms to break down the cells and release flavorful aromas and oils, and place them in a mug. Top with boiling water and allow to steep for at least 8 minutes, then serve as you would a regular cup of tea.

If you want to create a dried ingredient blend, which is great for storing, you need to dry out the leaves, seeds or roots first (dried licorice, ginger, chicory or fennel roots, for example, are great to add to dry blends). There are a variety of methods to accomplish this. When drying ingredients, you need to take larger cuttings, usually the whole stalk or root of the plant. You then either spread them on trays or tie them in bundles and leave them in a warm, well-ventilated place (such as an airing cupboard or kitchen cupboard). After around 5 days, remove the leaves or seeds and store them in an airtight container.

Another, much quicker, drying technique involves spreading leaves, seeds or roots out on a baking sheet lined with baking paper and placing them in the oven on a very low heat for around 4 hours. For the quickest and easiest method of drying ingredients, you can purchase a food dehydrator, though these can use a lot of power.

SCENTING TEA AT HOME

Scenting tea at home is easy but does require time and patience. You can either use an already scented tea, such as smoky lapsang souchong or floral jasmine tea, to blend with and scent other teas, or you can use aromatic ingredients such as flower petals, vanilla pods or coffee beans to scent your own tea.

If you are going with a prescented tea, there is no end of combinations you could try, depending on whether you want to complement the flavors or contrast them. The process relies on some trial and error to figure out what works and what you like, so it is best to blend in smaller quantities and keep notes as you go along.

If you would like to use your own ingredients to scent tea leaves, the best tea base for scenting is a good-quality but mellow tea such as a whole-leaf black Ceylon or Chinese green. These types of tea absorb the aroma well and are subtle enough to not override your scenting flavors. Good scenting ingredients to use are apples,

citrus peel or oil, vanilla beans or essence, coffee beans, fresh or dried flower petals, star anise and chilli.

To scent tea, using either of the above options, you will need to mix the leaves gently with the blending ingredient, or other scented tea leaves, and place in an airtight container for at least 48 hours. You can leave the mixture longer if you wish and you can leave the scenting ingredients in the blend completely, rather than removing them before brewing the tea, should you desire. Be aware, though, when using a fresh ingredient rather than a dried one, that it will need to be separated from your blend once the blend is scented, otherwise it will decay in the container over time. The simplest way to do this is to put the blending ingredient into a muslin sac so it is easily removed from the blend. Whichever way you choose to scent your tea, the result will be delicious.

SIX-STEP TEA BLENDING

Before you start blending, consider whether you want to blend for a particular health benefit or simply for flavor. If you want your blend to have a particular health benefit, do some research into ingredients that are aimed at boosting that particular area of health.

If you are blending for flavor, consider what sort of tastes and aromas you would like to achieve — fruity, spiced or floral, for example — and whether you would like to create a complementing blend or a contrasting blend. To achieve floral flavors, great complementary ingredients would be petals, such as rose or jasmine, or whole flowers, such as chamomile or lavender. To achieve a unique contrast with floral flavors you could match your floral base with sweet flavors, like coconut, or spices such as cardamom or cinnamon.

Once you have an idea you can begin. Bear in mind that tea blending can be a matter of experimenting, so blend in small batches and try your teas as you go along, adjusting where necessary. This is all part of the fun!

INGREDIENTS

Base tea

A particular variety of tea, a type of herb or a plant, like rooibos

Blending herbs

Fresh or dried herbs such as chamomile, peppermint, hibiscus, ginger or rose; spices such as cinnamon, cardamom, cloves

Inclusions

Dried flowers; dried fruit, such as citrus peel or berries

Scent

Fresh blossoms, essential oils

1. Add 5 teaspoons of base tea to a zipper-locked pouch or tin. The base tea is going to be your main ingredient and can be a particular tea, say, Assam, or it might be a herb, such as chamomile.

2. Choose a blending herb and add 1 heaped teaspoon to the base. This blending herb is going to be the most prominent element and you can increase the amount if you desire a stronger flavor.

3. Choose a second and, if you want, third blending herb and add 1 heaped teaspoon to the base. Identify your key flavor notes and consider which blending herbs will complement each other, say, floral flavors or fruity notes. As a general rule, don't use more than three blending herbs, as keeping it simple usually works best.

5. If scenting the tea, add the scent and leave the tea in an airtight, dry, cool place for at least 48 hours.

4. Add inclusions, if desired, and mix well. Inclusions won't add flavor to your blend but can be added for aesthetics or health benefits.

6. Taste your tea and tweak your recipe until you are happy with it.

BASE TEA
+
BLENDING HERB 1
+
BLENDING HERB 2 /INCLUSION/SCENT
+
INCLUSION/SCENT

A FEW BLENDING IDEAS

SPICED ORANGE CHAI

5 teaspoons black tea of choice
1 teaspoon cloves
1 teaspoon cardamom pods
1 teaspoon roughly chopped dried ginger
1 teaspoon chopped, dried orange peel

Other base options: Rooibos tea or yerba mate
Other blending options: Add 1 teaspoon cacao nibs
for a chocolate note or ½ teaspoon roughly chopped
cinnamon sticks for a special twist.

LAVENDER COCO-LICIOUS ROOIBOS

5 teaspoons rooibos tea
1 teaspoon dried lavender flowers
1 teaspoon desiccated coconut
1 teaspoon cacao nibs

Other base options: Chamomile, green or black tea
Other options: Try adding 1 teaspoon of dried chamomile
and/or dried rose petals for a further floral note.

WAKE-UP GARDEN BLEND

5 teaspoons green tea of choice
2 teaspoons dried or fresh lemongrass,
   chopped or sliced
1 teaspoon dried or fresh lemon thyme leaves
1 teaspoon dried or fresh rose petals
1 teaspoon dried or fresh hibiscus flower petals

Other base options: Rooibos, peppermint, chamomile,
green tea blend of choice
Other options: Add ½ teaspoon of dried chamomile
and/or dried lavender flowers for a further floral note or
1 teaspoon dried cinnamon for a gentle spice.

GREEN MINT GOJI

3 teaspoons green tea of choice
3 teaspoons fresh or dried mint leaves
1 teaspoon goji berries
1 teaspoon fresh or dried rose petals
1 teaspoon fresh or dried hibiscus flower petals

Other base options: peppermint, chamomile, lemongrass
Other options: For more cooling mint than fruity berry
flavor, omit the hibiscus and increase the mint to taste.

Opposite: A street vendor blends tea leaves, dried fruits and
herbs to make tea in the ancient city of Kashgar, the westernmost
city in China.

TEA MIXOLOGY

Tea is a fantastic ingredient for many types of drink and food, from steaming tea lattes to a perfectly baked spiced chai loaf. Perhaps the most common tea-based recipes are a traditional sweet iced tea and afternoon tea cake. It would be a shame to stop at these classics, though, as the versatility of tea makes it such an enjoyable and effortless ingredient to work with in the kitchen.

Functional foods — that is to say, foods that have additional health benefits above and beyond their nutritional content — have also become a big trend over the last few years. Mixing tea, with its high antioxidant levels, into all kinds of food and drink has become an exciting prospect.

From matcha tea cocktails and Earl Grey poached pears to lapsang-smoked salmon and super tea smoothies, tea is adding a new dimension to contemporary recipes. Below are a few tea-based recipes for you to enjoy at home.

ICED TEA

Iced tea was created in the United States in the 1800s as a way of enjoying tea in warmer climates, particularly in the southern states. Iced tea is typically taken very sweet and sometimes with the addition of lemon, peach or mint. When made the proper way, iced tea comprises freshly brewed tea leaves mixed with sugar and poured over ice, to which you can then add fresh fruit or a fruit syrup. It is also common to find bottled iced tea on the shelves of supermarkets all over the world, but be warned — there might not be any actual tea in there at all.

There are a few methods for making iced tea, depending on how quickly you want to prepare it.

If you are preparing iced tea in advance you can just brew it as you would hot tea, then let it cool down and place it in the fridge to chill.

If you want to make instant iced tea, you can use twice as much tea as usual in half the amount of hot water, then pour it over a cup or pitcher full of ice. As the ice melts, it dilutes the strong-brewed tea and also cools it down.

Lastly, there are a variety of methods for making cold-brewed tea, including so-called "sun brewing." This is where the tea leaves are infused in cool water rather than hot and they are left for an extended period of time to steep. The cooler temperature of the water tends to bring out the sweeter flavor compounds as well as more of the nutrients and antioxidants.

SIMPLE ICED TEA
Makes 1 glass

Brew **2 heaped teaspoons loose-leaf, or 2 teabags, of black tea** of your choice in **7 fl. oz. (200 ml) hot water** for 5 minutes. Sweeten with **honey, sugar or sweetener**, to taste, if desired. Pour into a large glass filled with ice cubes (if using loose-leaf tea, strain it into the glass).

Variations: to make flavored iced tea you can use a flavored tea, such as lemon green tea, as your base. Alternatively, you can add lemon juice and/or slices of lemon to regular green tea once it has cooled over ice in the serving glass. You can also create a simple sugar syrup by dissolving a cup of sugar in half a cup of water in a saucepan over a medium heat. Let it cool, then add a few drops of fruit juice, some puréed fruit or your favorite fruit flavoring and mix into the iced tea before serving.

For a refreshing glass of iced tea, simply pour strong, freshly brewed tea over ice cubes.

MATCHA

Matcha is a traditional Japanese powdered tea made from finely ground green tea leaves. The powder is prepared by whisking it with hot water to create a moderately thick beverage that is traditionally drunk in one go. Matcha has been enjoyed for hundreds of years as part of the Japanese tea ceremony, originally for its ability to help the monks leading the ceremonies to keep alert during their meditation and fasting. As you consume the whole of the tea leaf when drinking matcha, you ingest all of the caffeine, minerals and antioxidants, making matcha a potent superfood. See pages 56–57 and 218 for more about matcha.

Matcha can be a fabulous ingredient to jazz up many recipes. Try matcha in ice cream, sugar biscuits, buttercream and sponge mixes. It is also a great addition to smoothies and cocktails.

Matcha tea is traditionally prepared using a *chasen* — a Japanese bamboo whisk.

TO PREPARE MATCHA

Makes 1 cup

Place ½ **teaspoon of matcha powder** in a small bowl. Pour **1 fl. oz. (25 ml) cool water** into the bowl, then add **2½ fl. oz. (75 ml) hot water**. Using a bamboo whisk, whisk lightly, sweeping around the edge and the bottom of the bowl to remove any clumps sticking to the sides of the bowl. Then whisk using a "W" motion until a froth appears on the surface. (If you don't have a bamboo whisk. you can use a fork or handheld battery-operated whisk, though you will not be able to produce the highest-quality matcha.)

Rinse the whisk well, then enjoy your matcha straight from the bowl.

Variation: if you would like to enjoy a thinner matcha, as is sometimes the case after meals in Japan, you can top up the matcha with 7 fl. oz. (200 ml) hot water once whisked.

To make a matcha tea latte, pour in frothed milk and sprinkle with matcha powder to finish.

CHAI

In the streets of India, spiced black tea, or chai, is traditionally enjoyed very milky and very sweet. To make your own chai tea you can either do it the traditional way and brew your tea leaves in milk with a mixture of spices, as described here, or you can cheat slightly by adding sweetened steamed milk to your favorite chai tea blend, which is quicker (see below).

TO MAKE TRADITIONAL CHAI TEA
Makes 2 mugs

Place **14 fl. oz. (400 ml) whole milk** in a medium-sized saucepan. **Add 7 fl. oz. (200 ml) water**.

Add **3 teaspoons of loose-leaf black tea** or 3 black tea teabags and **chai spices** (you can use any variation of spices you like but a basic chai base would be: 1 stick of cinnamon, 4 crushed cardamom pods, 4 cloves, 1 in. (2.5 cm) piece fresh ginger, peeled and sliced, ½ teaspoon peppercorns) and simmer for 10 minutes. Add **2 teaspoons rock sugar, honey or brown sugar** and simmer for a further 3 minutes. Strain and serve.

TEA LATTES

Since the coffee boom, everybody is familiar with the idea of a coffee latte and many people would admit to it being their daily treat. The sweet, creamy flavors balance out the strength of the coffee and you can customize your drink by adding various flavored syrups. But it isn't just coffee that can be enjoyed as a tasty latte. In fact, "latte" means "steamed milk," so if you replace a coffee shot with tea you can enjoy a much healthier (and tastier) drink. You can make a tea latte from any of your favorite teas but there are a few teas that are particularly suited to enjoying with sweet steamed milk — chai and matcha, for example. You can find these beverages featured on menus worldwide as their popularity grows.

TO MAKE A CHAI TEA LATTE
Makes 1 mug

To make a chai latte, infuse **your favorite chai tea blend or teabag in 7 fl. oz. (200 ml) boiling water** for 6 minutes. Meanwhile, add **two teaspoons of honey or sugar** to **7 fl. oz. (200 ml) whole milk** and froth, using a steam wand, milk frother or handheld electric whisk. Pour the frothed milk onto the chai tea, leaving a frothy dollop on the top. Sprinkle with ground nutmeg or cinnamon to finish.

TO MAKE A MATCHA TEA LATTE
Makes 1 mug

As described on the opposite page, matcha is a great ingredient in all types of recipes. One of the simplest ways to enjoy matcha is as a tea latte. The slightly sweet, frothed milk adds an interesting creamy twist to the vegetal green tea notes. This recipe in particular tends to appeal to people who would love to enjoy matcha regularly but aren't too keen on its heavy flavors.

Prepare **3½ fl. oz. (100 ml) matcha tea** using the recipe on page 118. Froth **7 fl. oz. (200 ml) whole milk**, using a steam wand, milk frother or handheld electric whisk. (You can also use almond milk or add 2 teaspoons of honey or sugar to the milk to sweeten it, if desired.) Pour the milk onto the freshly brewed matcha, leaving a frothy dollop on the top. Sprinkle with matcha powder to finish.

A street vendor pushes a bicycle laden with cups, teapots and other household goods down a street in Hanoi. Vietnam has an ideal climate for tea cultivation, and the country's tea industry has huge potential for growth.

PART FOUR

THE WORLD OF TEA

AFRICA

Africa is a fairly new to tea production but its growth, especially in East African countries, has been rapid over the last 50 years. After Asia, Africa produces the second highest amount of tea in the world and a huge 62 percent of this is produced in Kenya alone. As a percentage, Africa exports the largest amount of the tea it produces each year and, combined, African tea growers contribute 12 percent of the world's tea production. Africa is also unique in leading the black CTC market, which produces teas that are rich and full bodied in flavor. These teas are meant to be enjoyed as breakfast-style teas, taken with milk, and are mostly exported for the European, Middle East and North American markets.

TEA-PRODUCING COUNTRIES

(IN ORDER OF PRODUCTION VOLUME)

KENYA

By far Africa's largest producer of tea and the third largest producer of tea in the world, Kenya is the world leader in CTC black tea and makes up 22 percent of the world's exports of tea. Many other tea-producing African countries export their teas through Kenya's weekly auctions, which are held in Mombasa.

Produces: 476,640 tons (432,400 tonnes)
Exports: 258,140 tons (234,180 tonnes)
Imports: 95,785 tons (86,895 tonnes)
Consumes: 89,570 tons (81,255 tonnes)
Annual consumption per person: 4.4 lb. (2 kg)
Tea profile: Strong, full-bodied, coppery CTC black teas. Small amount of white tea.

MALAWI

The first tea in Africa was planted in Malawi in the late 1800s. After Kenya, Malawi is Africa's second largest tea producer and, like Kenya, its teas are mostly used in black tea blends. Some premium teas are produced on specialty farms in Malawi, but in general its unpredictable weather and less than ideal tea-growing climate mean that most Malawian teas fetch a fairly low price at auction. Recently, Malawi has been researching and testing new clones of tea saplings in an attempt to find a hybrid more suitable to its climate.

Produces: 59,525 tons (54,000 tonnes)
Exports: 38,225 tons (34,680 tonnes)
Imports: 65 tons (60 tonnes)
Consumes: 6,615 tons (6,000 tonnes)
Annual consumption per person: 14 oz. (400 g)
Tea profile: Strong, full-bodied, coppery CTC black teas. Small amount of white tea.

Previous pages: At almost 10,000 ft. (3,000 m), Mount Mulanje towers over the Mulanje tea-growing region in southern Malawi.

Red Sea

SUDAN

ERITREA

CHAD

Blue Nile

White Nile

Gulf of Aden

DJIBOUTI

NIGERIA

CAMEROON

Benue

CENTRAL
AFRICAN
REPUBLIC

SOUTH
SUDAN

Addis
Ababa

Dire
Dawa

ETHIOPIA

SOMALIA

Douala

Yaoundé

Ubangi

Congo

Mbandaka

Kisangani

UGANDA

Lake
Turkana

Gulf of Guinea

GABON

CONGO

DEMOCRATIC

REPUBLIC

Kampala

Kisumu

KENYA

Lake
Victoria

Kigali

RWANDA

Nairobi

Kinshasa

OF THE

CONGO

Bujumbura

BURUNDI

Mbuji-Mayi

Lake
Tanganyika

Mombasa

Dodoma

Dar Es Salaam

INDIAN
OCEAN

TANZANIA

ATLANTIC
OCEAN

Lubumbashi

MALAWI

ANGOLA

Lake Nyasa
(L. Malawi)

ZAMBIA

Zambezi

MOZAMBIQUE

Mozambique Channel

MADAGASCAR

Harare

ZIMBABWE

Beira

N

Bulawayo

0   miles   500

BOTSWANA

Limpopo

0   km   500

Maputo

SWAZILAND

PRODUCES: 770,580 tons (699,055 tonnes)

IMPORTS: 434,000 tons (393,720 tonnes)

EXPORTS: 453,375 tons (411,295 tonnes)

CONSUMES: 553,205 tons (501,860 tonnes)

ANNUAL CONSUMPTION PER PERSON:
1 lb. 3 oz. (530 g)

UGANDA

Tea production in Uganda forms a large part of the country's exports but it has seen many knock-backs including war, labor shortages, low yields and debt. The climate and terrain are good for tea production and production has increased 15-fold since the 1980s but the above challenges have left the tea quality poor. For this reason, Ugandan tea is rarely enjoyed pure outside its local market and it is often sold to Kenya, where it is added as a filler to their higher-quality blends.

Produces: 58,420 tons (53,000 tonnes)
Exports: 55,115 tons (50,000 tonnes)
Imports: 385 tons (350 tonnes)
Consumes: 1,985 tons (1,800 tonnes)
Annual consumption per person: 2 oz. (50 g)
Tea profile: Strong, full-bodied but inconsistent CTC black teas often sold to be combined with higher-quality Kenyan teas

BURUNDI

Production may have started late, in the 1970s, but Burundi teas fetch the second highest price of all East African counties, just above Kenyan teas. Tea is a major cash crop for Burundi and many plantations are run by rural villages, making tea a large source of employment also. Tea quality is high because the tropical climate and high hilly terrain provide an ideal environment for growing tea.

Produces: 46,095 tons (41,815 tonnes)
Exports: 10,690 tons (9,700 tonnes)
Imports: None
Consumes: No data
Annual consumption per person: No data
Tea profile: Strong but aromatic flavor

UNITED REPUBLIC OF TANZANIA

The Tanzanian tea industry suffers from vast inconsistency across the country and on average its teas fetch significantly lower price at auction, when compared to Kenyan and Rwandan teas, because of this inconsistency. Variability in harvesting and processing standards, as well as labor shortages, make production unreliable.

Produces: 37,150 tons (33,700 tonnes)
Exports: 29,875 tons (27,100 tonnes)
Imports: 65 tons (60 tonnes)
Consumes: 7,495 tons (6,800 tonnes)
Annual consumption per person: 5 oz. (140 g)
Tea profile: Strong CTC black teas, with complex fruity notes

MOZAMBIQUE

Black tea is produced mainly for the domestic market, but political unrest has disrupted production and has had an effect on the tea price at auction.

Produces: 25,355 tons (23,000 tonnes)
Exports: 2,755 tons (2,500 tonnes)
Imports: 275 tons (250 tonnes)
Consumes: 22,820 tons (20,700 tonnes)
Annual consumption per person: 1 lb. 12 oz. (800 g)
Tea profile: Strong, fragrant black teas

RWANDA

Teas produced by Rwanda's 11 tea estates currently fetch the highest price of all East African countries and they are in high demand for export. Climate and terrain are excellent, with plenty of rainfall and nutrient-rich soil. Yield has been low over the last 10 years due to political unrest but rehabilitation is in full swing.

Produces: 24,455 tons (22,185 tonnes)
Exports: 22,060 tons (20,010 tonnes)
Imports: 275 tons (250 tonnes)
Consumes: 2,755 tons (2,500 tonnes)
Annual consumption per person: 10 oz. (290 g)
Tea profile: High-quality CTC and orthodox black teas

ZIMBABWE

Tea production in Zimbabwe relies heavily on irrigation as annual rainfall is less than 24 in. (600 mm). There are two tea-growing regions: Chipping and Honde Valley.

Produces: 20,995 tons (19,000 tonnes)
Exports: 12,675 tons (11,500 tonnes)
Imports: 385 tons (350 tonnes)
Consumes: 8,380 tons (7,600 tonnes)
Annual consumption per person: 1 lb. 3 oz. (540 g)
Tea profile: Strong flavor with dark-colored liquor

ETHIOPIA

Ethiopian teas are grown in the south, near to the Kenyan border. Climate and terrain that are similar to those in Kenya means that Ethiopian teas are quickly catching up in terms of quality and flavor.

Produces: 8,155 tons (7,400 tonnes)
Exports: 350 tons (320 tonnes)
Imports: None
Consumes: 7,845 tons (7,120 tonnes)
Annual consumption per person: 3 oz. (80 g)
Tea profile: Strong, full-bodied flavor with deep liquor

CAMEROON

Cameroon has only three small tea-producing areas — in Tole (low altitude), Ndu (high altitude) and Djuttitsa — which produce very different-tasting teas, but all are of high quality.

Produces: 5,180 tons (4,700 tonnes)
Exports: None
Imports: 255 tons (230 tonnes)
Consumes: 5,180 tons (4,700 tonnes)
Annual consumption per person: 8 oz. (220 g)
Tea profile: Bright, good-flavored CTC black teas to be enjoyed with milk

DEMOCRATIC REPUBLIC OF THE CONGO

Tea-growing regions in the Democratic Republic of Congo are mostly on the Rwandan border, where the climate and terrain are particularly suitable and the elevation is high.

Produces: 3,195 tons (2,900 tonnes)
Exports: 70 tons (65 tonnes)
Imports: 200 tons (180 tonnes)
Consumes: 2,755 tons (2,500 tonnes)
Annual consumption per person: 9 oz. (250 g)
Tea profile: Bright, brisk black teas, both CTC and orthodox

Left: Tea packaged and ready for export at the Teza Tea Factory in Muramvya Province in central Burundi. Coffee and tea exports make up the majority of the country's foreign revenue.

KENYA

Kenya is the third largest producer of tea in the world, flying the flag for Africa in the very Asian-dominated tea industry. Of the nearly 771,615 tons (700,000 tonnes) of tea produced across the continent each year, Kenya alone produces 62 percent. As a percentage of what it produces, Kenya is the world's largest exporter of tea, accounting for a whopping 22 percent of the world tea export market. Not only that, Kenya is the world leader in producing the type of CTC teas perfect for making the full-bodied, black breakfast blends that are so popular in the major export markets in Europe, Canada, the Middle East and Japan.

Cultivation is split between two types of systems — small rural farms, called smallholdings (or *shambas*), and large company-run plantations. In terms of the smallholder model of tea production, Kenya is once again a world leader, although, as we will explore, this has its benefits and its failings.

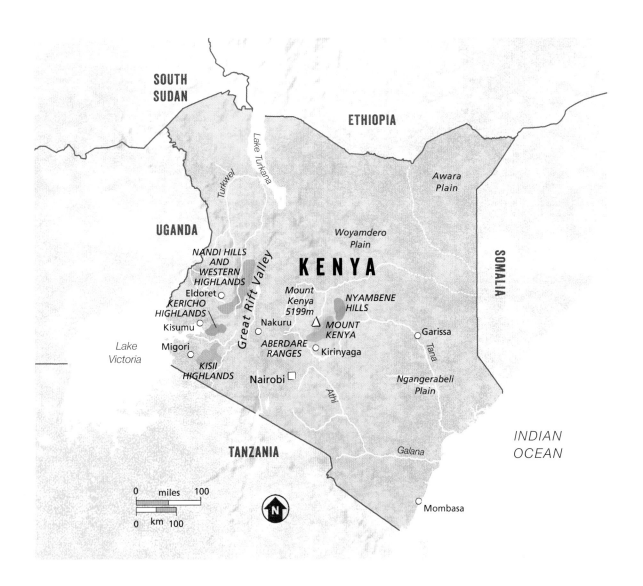

HISTORY AND DEVELOPMENT

Tea was first introduced to Kenya in the early 1900s when seeds from India were planted in the Highlands by the British brothers, the Caines. For many years the tea industry in Kenya was owned and controlled by colonial and foreign powers and it wasn't until independence in 1963 that laws were passed and the Kenya Tea Development Authority (KTDA) was formed to support and encourage Kenyan farmers to cultivate their own tea farms.

By this time there was great potential for tea to become an important national export and many governing bodies were set up to control and promote the industry. These organizations have put a lot of effort and resources into using any suitable land for tea cultivation to maximize production and to ensure that quality is consistently high.

PRODUCES: 476,640 tons (432,400 tonnes)

EXPORTS: 258,140 tons (234,180 tonnes)

IMPORTS: 95,785 tons (86,895 tonnes)

CONSUMES: 89,570 tons (81,255 tonnes)

ANNUAL CONSUMPTION PER PERSON:
4 lb. (1.83 kg)

Opposite: A cool climate and soil that is rich in nutrients unite in the Abedare Ranges of Kenya to create conditions ideal for growing black tea.

Starting from those few small farms in the Highlands, Kenya now has the most smallholders in the world, spread over 170,500 acres (69,000 hectares), 13 tea-growing regions and over 60 factories — far surpassing the number of Kenya's company-owned plantations, although there are still many of these.

CLIMATE, TERRAIN AND HARVESTING

The majority of Kenya's tea-growing regions are found in the Kenyan Highlands, on both sides of the Great Rift Valley. This valley sits on the equator at an altitude of 4,900 to 8,860 ft. (1,500–2,700 m), and provides the ideal climate for tea growing: long, sunny days and consistent rainfall all year, combined with a very nutrient-rich, red volcanic soil. Tea is grown and harvested all year round.

Tea plucking and processing are still done by hand, using traditional methods, although some of the larger estates have machinery. The top two leaves and the bud are constantly plucked every week to 2 weeks throughout the year, but the best harvests are in late January and July.

Many smallholdings share a central factory that processes all the tea grown in their area and most factories are geared toward producing CTC black tea. Educational resources and guidelines regarding best

growing and harvesting practices are also shared among the smallholdings by the KTDA, which helps keep standards consistent and high countrywide.

The use of pesticides is regulated and rarely necessary but fertilizers are used on Kenya's red soils to replenish nutrients. This is mainly an organic fertilizer — the offcuts from pruning that are spread over the soil at the feet of the plants.

SMALLHOLDERS AND THE KTDA

There is no doubt that Kenya is leading the way for the smallholder tea-growing system, in numbers anyway.

Tea has become an important source of livelihood for small farmers all over the country and the central control of the KTDA ensures standards are maintained and prices at auction are just as high as those of estate-produced tea. The KTDA has also been able to implement partnerships with organizations like Rainforest Alliance (see page 68) and to give some ownership of factories and land back to the farmers.

Because tea is such a large national export, the tea industry in Kenya has the potential to positively affect the livelihood of all those working within it, many of whom live below the poverty line. However, it also has the potential to exploit those at the bottom of the supply chain as Kenya strives to keep up with worldwide demand.

Typically, working conditions have a bad reputation and the same centralized control takes away decision-making from the smallholders as they have little relationship with, or influence over, the final buyers of their tea. It also makes it hard for external charities and nongovernmental organizations (NGOs) to be able to step in and help. Although prices fetched at auction are fair and easily match those of the estate-produced teas, the KTDA charges administration fees to the smallholders, which means they are at a disadvantage.

The relationship between smallholders and the centrally owned and controlled factories can also be strained, as the farmers feel no ownership over the tea they have produced. However, in the last 5 years, ownership of the tea factories has started to be shared with local smallholders in some areas.

Left: Masai women in Kenya share a pot of tea. Tea consumption has grown steadily in the country, with the average person in Kenya now drinking about 4 lb (1.83 kg) each year.

REGIONS

ABERDARE RANGES

Tea type: Black CTC

Climate/terrain: Rolling hills, 5,575 to 7,220 ft. (1,700–2,200 m); cool forest climate; nutrient-rich soil

Location: 19 mi. (30 km) northwest of Nairobi

Factories: Kambaa, Mataara, Kagwe, Theta, Negere, Githambo

MOUNT KENYA

Tea type: Black CTC

Climate/terrain: 4,920 to 7,220 ft. (500–2,200 m); rich, volcanic soil; cool climate with good rainfall

Location: 94 mi. (152 km) northeast of Nairobi, on the southeastern slopes of Mount Kenya

Factories: Ndima, Kangaita, Mungania, Kimunye, Thumaita, Kathangariri

NYAMBENE HILLS

Tea type: Black CTC

Climate/terrain: 4,920 to 6,400 ft. (1,500–1,950 m); rich, clay-based soil, cool climate with good rainfall

Location: Central Kenya

Factories: Weru, Kinoro, Kionyo, Imenti, Githongo, Igembe, Michimikuru, Kiegoi

KERICHO HIGHLANDS

Tea type: Black CTC

Climate/terrain: 4,920 to 7,055 ft. (1,500–2,150 m); dual rainfall from Lake Victoria and the Mau Forest hits the area

Location: Between the Mau Forest and Kisii Highlands

Factories: Toror, Tegat, Momul, Litein, Chelal, Kapkatet, Mogogosiek, Kobel

KISII HIGHLANDS

Tea type: Black CTC

Climate/terrain: 4,920 to 7,055 ft. (1,500–2,150 m); Lake Victoria basin keeps it well watered; warm weather and mineral-rich soil

Location: West of Kericho Highlands toward Lake Victoria

Factories: Sanganyi, Tombe, Gianchore, Nyansiongo, Kebirigo, Nyankoba

NANDI HILLS AND WESTERN HIGHLANDS

Tea type: Black CTC, white tea

Climate/terrain: 5,250 to 6,560 ft. (1,600–2,000 m); warm weather, plenty of rainfall and mineral-rich soil

Location: West Kenya, on the equator, near the Kakamega Forest

Factories: Chebut, Kaptumo, Mudete, Kapsara, Olenguruone

TYPES OF TEA GROWN IN KENYA

Described as bright and brisk with a red-copper tint to the liquor, Kenyan teas are regularly sold in bulk to large blending houses to add to black breakfast tea blends. It is unusual to find single-estate Kenyan teas.

Kenyan teas are in high demand and fetch a good price at auction, especially compared to other African teas. The tea produced for blending in Kenya is CTC, full-bodied, bright in both color and flavor, and designed to be taken with milk. Kenya also produces a small amount of white and green teas.

SILVERBACK WHITE TEA

Region: Nandi

Climate/terrain: High elevation — 6,560 ft. (2,000 m); misty and moist, bright and long sunny days and nutrient-rich, red volcanic soil

Processing methods: Hand-plucked and gently dried; only 1,325 lb. (600 kg) is produced a year

Taste profile: Sweet, aromatic, honey notes, smooth mouthfeel

MILIMA BLACK TEA

Region: Kericho Highlands

Climate/terrain: 6,235 ft. (1,900 m); cool air and rocky soil

Processing methods: Orthodox tea production

Taste profile: Zesty, warm, slightly spiced aroma

Opposite, above: In Kenya, the tea industry is a key source of employment.
Opposite, below: Vendors at a market in the Old Town of Mombasa sell a variety of locally produced teas.

Workers at Mbaraki Port Warehouses Company in Mombasa load sacks of tea onto a conveyor belt. Tea is Kenya's main source of foreign-currency earnings, and weekly tea auctions are held in Mombasa, the country's chief port.

ROOIBOS TEA

Rooibos, or red bush, tea is a naturally caffeine-free beverage made from the leaves of the rooibos plant (*Aspalathus linearis*). The plant grows in South Africa and, once dried, has distinctive red leaves — hence both its Afrikaans and English names.

South Africans drink rooibos tea as the Chinese drink green or the British drink black teas — it is their everyday tea of choice. In addition to be being caffeine free, it has the added health benefits of being high in antioxidants and great for the skin. All these benefits have seen it grow in popularity across the world over the last few years. Many people class rooibos tea as herbal tea and it is a great ingredient to blend with, as it goes well with all sorts of flavors (see page 110).

HOW IS IT MADE AND SERVED

Rooibos tea is made by infusing the dried leaves in boiling water for at least 4 minutes. Traditionally, rooibos is prepared as a loose-leaf tea but you can now find teabags, too. Unlike typical teas made from the *Camellia sinensis* plant, you cannot really over-brew rooibos and it will never become bitter if oversteeped.

In fact, rooibos is a very versatile tea, perhaps another reason why it is growing in popularity. It has a slightly nutty, earthy taste and a deep-red liquor that goes well with milk and sugar, as well as without.

The malty flavor of rooibos makes it a great alternative to coffee, especially when made into a tea latte, with the addition of honey and frothy milk (see page 119).

GROWING, HARVESTING AND PROCESSING

Rooibos is grown, harvested and processed in a very similar way to tea but it only comes in two types: red and green.

Red rooibos is the most common and fully oxidized version, whereas green rooibos isn't oxidized, similar to green teas, so retains its green appearance. Green rooibos tastes grassier and vegetal, similar to yerba mate or chamomile, whereas red rooibos tastes malty and a little earthy, like black teas.

HISTORY

Rooibos has been being produced in South Africa for hundreds of years and is enjoyed by visitors and locals alike. Unlike tea, rooibos didn't become a popular commodity to trade so it remained fairly unknown outside of South Africa for most of the 18th to 20th centuries.

More recently, the growth of rooibos tea's popularity has been one of the largest in the tea industry and it is now easy to find a range of rooibos teas in your local supermarket.

Opposite, above: Rooibos tea leaves are harvested by hand with sickles, then bound into neat bundles for processing.

Opposite, below: Farm workers sweep up sun-dried rooibos leaves in the Cedarberg region of South Africa's Western Cape. South Africa is the only country in the world to grow rooibos tea.

INDIAN SUBCONTINENT

The Indian subcontinent is home to some of the largest players in the tea industry, as well as some of the world's biggest tea lovers — India and Sri Lanka both feature on the top 10 producers list. The *assamica* variety of the tea plant is native to the Himalayan region of India, and tea has been cultivated successfully on a commercial scale since the region was under British colonial rule in the 19th century. The desire to set up tea plantations to meet drinking demands in Europe, rather than rely on importing from China, drove the birth of a fantastic industry that would go on to help define the whole subcontinent.

TEA-PRODUCING COUNTRIES

(IN ORDER OF PRODUCTION VOLUME)

INDIA

By far the region's largest producer of tea and the second largest in the world, India produces a wide variety of black teas, many of which are world renowned and highly sought after. Indian teas are harvested seasonally and it is common to find teas named after the region in which they are grown, the time of harvest and the grade of the tea.

Produces: 1,332,450 tons (1,208,780 tonnes)
Exports: 248,110 tons (225,080 tonnes)
Imports: 23,430 tons (21,255 tonnes)
Consumes: 1,059,770 tons (961,410 tonnes)
Annual consumption per person: 1 lb. 11 oz. (770 g)
Tea profile: Wide variety of black teas, the most famous being from the Darjeeling, Assam and Nilgiri areas

SRI LANKA

Although Sri Lanka is small compared to other countries in the region, its tea industry is deeply ingrained in the country's society and economy, and is the fourth largest in the world, in terms of production. The majority of Sri Lanka's teas are produced for the export market, which is strong in the Middle East, Europe and Japan.

Produces: 375,060 tons (340,250 tonnes)
Exports: 350,865 tons (318,300 tonnes)
Imports: 7,385 tons (6,700 tonnes)
Consumes: 30,425 tons (27,600 tonnes)
Annual consumption per person: 1 lb. 14 oz. (1.3 kg)
Tea profile: Wide variety of black teas with some green and white also. Teas are known by the height of elevation at which they are grown — low-, mid- and high-country teas are grown.

Previous pages: Tea is a major industry in Bangladesh, growing in regions including Sylhet, which has over 150 tea gardens such as the one shown here.

CHINA

PAKISTAN

Thar Desert

HIMALAYA

NEPAL

□ Kathmandu

BHUTAN

Delhi ○ □ New Delhi

Faridabad ○

Yamuna

Ganges Plain

Agra ○ ○ Lucknow

Ganges

○ Patna

○ Varanasi

Ganges

Brahmaputra

BANGLADESH

BURMA (MYANMAR)

Ahmadabad ○

Vindhya Range

Narmada

Satpura Range

Nagpur ○

Mahanadi

Kolkata ○

Bay of Bengal

I N D I A

D e c c a n

Arabian Sea

Mumbai ○

Pune ○

Godavari

Hyderabad ○

Western Ghats

Eastern Ghats

INDIAN OCEAN

Chennai ○

Bangalore ○

INDIAN OCEAN

Kochi ○

N

| 0 | miles | 300 |
| 0 | km | 300 |

SRI LANKA

Colombo □

PRODUCES: 1,800,755 tons (1,633,620 tonnes)

EXPORTS: 611,235 tons (554,500 tonnes)

IMPORTS: 31,980 tons (29,010 tonnes)

CONSUMES: 1,165,494 tons (1,057,318 tonnes)

ANNUAL CONSUMPTION PER PERSON:
3 lb. 5 oz. (1.5 kg)

BANGLADESH

Tea spread into Bangladesh in the 1800s from the Assam region in India. There has been a strong industry since, although exports have all but died out.

Produces: 70,550 tons (64,000 tonnes)
Exports: 925 tons (840 tonnes)
Imports: 745 tons (675 tonnes)
Consumes: 64,705 tons (58,700 tonnes)
Annual consumption per person: 13 oz. (380 g)
Tea profile: Strong, fragrant black teas, great with milk

NEPAL

Tea is grown in Nepal in the valleys of the Himalayas, where the climate is suited to tea production. There is large interest in tea from the domestic market but more recently single-estate Nepalese teas have been gaining popularity further afield. This has seen a healthy spike in export opportunities.

Produces: 22,695 tons (20,590 tonnes)
Exports: 11,335 tons (10,280 tonnes)
Imports: 420 tons (380 tonnes)
Consumes: 10,490 tons (9,610 tonnes)
Annual consumption per person: 12 oz. (350 g)
Tea profile: High-quality orthodox black teas

Left: Women, who make up over 75 percent of the tea workforce in Bangladesh, carry tea leaves on their backs at a tea garden in Moulvibazar District.

INDIA

The largest consumers of tea in the world, the Indian people get through 23 percent of the world's tea every year — well over two billion cups of tea a day! India is also the world's second largest producer of tea, which is remarkable considering the plants lie dormant over winter, unlike those in many other countries where tea can be harvested all year round. Although native to India, the tea plant wasn't really used there in beverages, other than for medicinal purposes, until the 19th century. The country was under the rule of the British Empire at this time, and large-scale tea plantations were first cultivated to serve the British nation's rapidly growing tea habit. As black tea became readily available across India, it also started

Above: A *chaiwallah*, or chai vendor, pours glasses of freshly made masala chai, a sweet, milky and aromatic tea-based beverage popular throughout India.

PRODUCES:	1,332,450 tons (1,208,780 tonnes)
EXPORTS:	248,110 tons (225,080 tonnes)
IMPORTS:	23,430 tons (21,255 tonnes)
CONSUMES:	1,059,770 tons (961,410 tonnes)
ANNUAL CONSUMPTION PER PERSON:	1 lb. 11 oz. (770 g)

finding its way into domestic recipes, such as traditional masala chai. This blend of tea, spices and sweet milk quickly became the staple of the Indian people, to help with everything from cooling down in the heat, warming up in the cool evenings and staying awake during long journeys (see page 119 for a recipe).

HISTORY AND DEVELOPMENT

The *assamica* variety of the tea plant has grown wild in India for thousands of years and the Indian people have been making tea from it for at least 500 years. During the colonial era in India tea production was a key focus of the British Empire, whose authorities saw its vast capital-earning potential. Starting from some small botanical gardens in Kolkata (formerly Calcutta), a booming industry developed and, by the time India gained independence in 1947, it was producing nearly 330,690 tons (300,000 tonnes) a year.

Tea is responsible for the livelihoods of over three million people, spread across 20 states and 12,800 tea farms and estates.

Until the early 21st century India was the main producer of tea worldwide, but in the last few years growth in the Chinese industry has seen it outstrip India's production.

India's tea industry is interesting as it produces on a large scale to support both domestic demand and the export market, covering mass-market black teas for breakfast blends and also higher-quality specialty single-estate teas that have such a reputation worldwide. This reputation has led the Indian Tea Board to create quality guarantees to ensure that only teas grown and produced to the highest levels in either Darjeeling or Assam are labeled as such.

CLIMATE, TERRAIN AND HARVESTING

It is the climate of the famous tea regions of Assam and Darjeeling that is considered the key to producing such exquisite flavors of tea. The complex balance of conditions throughout the whole year come together perfectly during one or two harvests a year, producing much sought-after aromas and flavors in the tea produced. These teas are in high demand by India's export countries and they fetch a premium at market.

The different harvests are referred to as "flushes," the first flush usually being the first of the season, in early spring. At this point there is some rainfall but the air is still quite dry from the winter. Second flush tends to take place in early summer, June perhaps, when the higher amount of rainfall means that the harvested teas are good quality. There is sometimes then the monsoon tea, or in-between tea, which is any tea harvested throughout the heavy rains of the mid-season.

Left: A man carries a portable chai stand at a camel fair in Rajasthan. The chai is served in a kind of handle-less terracotta cup called a *kulhud*.

Opposite: Freshly picked leaves are loaded onto a trailer at a tea plantation in Kerala, a region of India that produces large quantities of green tea.

REGIONS

Tea is produced in nearly 20 Indian states, but the majority of these are in the north, in the foothills of the Himalayas. Some tea is also produced around the northern edges of New Delhi and also around the southern Nilgiri Mountains. The main tea regions, in more detail, are:

ASSAM

Tea type: Assam black teas — various flushes

Climate/terrain: High altitude mountains and valleys, sheltered by the Himalayan Mountains; high rainfall, especially during the monsoon season; very humid, especially during the rainy season

Location: Brahmaputra Valley, 120 mi. (193 km) east of Darjeeling, bordering China, Burma (Myanmar) and Bangladesh

Tea farms/plantations: Bamonpookri, Napuk, Thowra, Khongea

DARJEELING

Tea type: Darjeeling black teas — various flushes

Climate/terrain: High altitude; seasonal rains; cool, dry air but with misty periods

Location: Northeast India, West Bengal, foot of the Himalayas

Tea farms/plantations: Castleton, Bloomfield, Puttabong, Makaibari

NILGIRI MOUNTAINS

Tea type: Black and green teas

Climate/terrain: High altitude, 5,900 ft. (1,800 m); grassy plains and jungle; plenty of irrigation and nutrient-rich soil from rivers, and two distinct monsoon seasons

Location: Southwest tip of India

Tea farms/plantations: Glendale, Tigerhill, Tungmullay, Havukal

HIMACHAL PRADESH

Tea type: Green, black and oolong teas

Climate/terrain: Mountainous, high altitude; very wet

Location: Northwest India

Tea farms/plantations: Kangra

SIKKIM

Tea type: Black teas, similar to Darjeeling in aroma and flavor

Climate/terrain: High altitude, mountainous; seasonal rains; cool, dry air and subtropical climate; some mist

Location: Just above Darjeeling in northeast India

Tea farms/plantations: Temi, Glenburn

KERALA

Tea type: Green, white teas

Climate/terrain: Similar to Nilgiri as it lies in the same mountain range

Location: Southernmost tip of southwest India

Tea farms/plantations: Oothu, Kolukkumalai

CHALLENGES TO THE ASSAM REGION

Assam is not only India's largest tea-producing region, it is also the world's largest, with over 2,000 tea farms. The region is world renowned for the quality of the tea it produces and there is a strong market for both its higher-quality single-estate version and the CTC grades for blending into black breakfast teas.

However, this famous tea region faces some challenges that threaten its future. First, political instability in the area disrupts production, investment and trade, and has caused seasonal labor shortages. Second, a flood of countries producing CTC black teas has meant the price has dropped dramatically, causing nearly 200 tea gardens to close in Assam since the beginning of the century.

TYPES OF TEA GROWN IN INDIA

India mostly produces black teas, split between CTC and orthodox production, but it has started to produce some whites, greens and oolongs more recently. India is the largest producer of CTC teas, contributing a significant 60 percent of the world's supply.

Much like Sri Lanka, India follows the British grading system (see page 25) and can alter production methods to create different teas at different times to suit the market demands. India also uses the "first flush, second flush" (see page 148) notification to indicate the harvest from which the tea was plucked and teas are often named after the estate or region in which they were produced. Regardless of market trends, three of India's teas are world famous and always in demand — Assam, Darjeeling and Nilgiri.

ASSAM

Found as either first flush, second flush or a blend

Region: Assam

Climate/terrain: High altitude, misty mountains

Processing methods: Highest-quality harvested in second flush, May to June

Taste profile: Strong, full-bodied, malty flavor with deep-red liquor

DARJEELING

Found as either first flush, second flush or a blend

Region: Darjeeling, West Bengal

Climate/terrain: High altitude; seasonal weather system that creates the unique, famous "Darjeeling flavor"

Processing methods: Various genetic mixes of tea plant found across the Darjeeling area. Normal black tea processing but the dry, cool, high-altitude — thus thinner — air helps to speed up the drying stage, resulting in the lightness that is unique to Darjeeling teas.

Taste profile: Light, aromatic, "champagne" flavor; best without milk

NILGIRI

Region: Nilgiri Mountains, southwest India

Climate/terrain: Jungle-faced mountains and large areas of grassland with high monsoon rainfall; warm, moist conditions

Processing methods: Harvesting takes place all year round, uniquely including in the middle of winter when the harvest is used to make "frost tea."

Taste profile: Strong and dark but smooth, fragrant and well-rounded. Frost tea is sweet and fruity.

TEMI

Region: Skikkim, north India

Climate/terrain: High altitude; unique seasonal weather system

Processing methods: Normal black tea processing and similarities to Darjeeling region result in similar lightness in Temi teas

Taste profile: Light, aromatic, best without milk

TULSI

Tulsi (*Ocimum tenuiflorum*) is a herb that grows in India and is nicknamed "holy basil" because of its variety of health, healing and religious uses. It is considered an Ayurvedic herb (see page 107) and has been used to make herbal teas in the Indian subcontinent for generations. Tulsi has a slight grassy, floral and citrus flavor and can have a sweet aftertaste when enjoyed pure. Tulsi is often used as a blending ingredient to add to other herbal or tea-based hot drinks.

Tea pickers wait patiently to have their sacks of leaves weighed amid lush green tea bushes at this plantation in Kerala, southern India. Many tea pickers will harvest at least 90 lb. (40 kg) of leaves per day.

SRI LANKA

The island nation of Sri Lanka, formerly Ceylon, exports 94 percent of the tea it grows — the largest percentage in the world. It is also the fourth highest producer of tea worldwide, and is unique in that it can produce tea throughout the whole year.

Most of the tea plantations of Sri Lanka produce black teas and can be found in the centrally located hill country, where the warm climate, high altitude and sloped terrain combine to provide the perfect conditions for tea production. Most of Sri Lanka's export market is in the Middle East and Europe but there are also plenty of bidders worldwide for its specialty high-country grown Nuwara Eliya teas.

Above: One of the most picturesque tea estates in Sri Lanka, the Kataboola Estate has acres of tea grown on rolling mountains and surrounded by patches of verdant forest.

HISTORY AND DEVELOPMENT

Much as in India, tea was first introduced to Sri Lanka during its time under British rule in the 19th century. Exploring the island, the British soon saw there was huge agricultural potential in the thousands of acres of untouched jungle land that lay in the mountainous hill country. Originally, the land was cleared in order for coffee plantations to be set up, but these plantations were quickly converted to tea estates after the coffee plants suffered a crippling crop disease and the British realized that tea plants were much better suited to the climate and terrain than coffee — and that tea, as well as rubber, would be much more profitable.

Loolecondera, the first tea estate in Sri Lanka, was established in 1867 by James Taylor, who saw an opportunity to supply tea to the United Kingdom. Many other British entrepreneurs were quick to recognize the country's potential and set up their own tea plantations, including the famous Thomas Lipton. Another was George Thomson, who set up the Newburgh Estate in Uva in the early 1900s. A large majority of the factories and estates in Sri Lanka have British origins and some are still British owned and run.

Compared to other tea-producing countries, Sri Lanka exports a significant amount of the tea it produces, to the value of nearly US$3 billion. It is not surprising then that 5 percent of the country's population — more than a million people — work in the tea industry in some way. Sri Lanka has also set up its own tea board and developed its own brand and logo, "Ceylon" tea, with the red lion as its mascot. The Sri Lankan Tea Board has helped ensure that many of the big tea brands, like Liptons and Tetleys, choose to have their teas packaged, as well as produced, in Sri Lanka. The quality of teas blended and packaged in Sri Lanka is consistently high, making them the largest producer of fully packaged teas in the world.

CLIMATE, TERRAIN AND HARVESTING

Tea-growing regions in Sri Lanka are grouped into areas denoted by elevation — low country (sea level to 2,000 ft./600 m), mid-country 2,000 to 4,000 ft. (600–1,200 m) and high country 4,000 ft. (1,200 m). Each region has a different climate and terrain, and they are known for producing their own, distinct flavors of tea. More than 40 percent of Sri Lankan tea is low-country grown, 27 percent is mid-country and 33 percent is high-country grown.

In the mid- and high regions, tea plantations are spread across hillside terraces, often with a factory sitting atop one of the hills. In the low country, it is not

PRODUCES:	375,040 tons (340,230 tonnes)
EXPORTS:	350,865 tons (318,300 tonnes)
IMPORTS:	7,385 tons (6,700 tonnes)
CONSUMES:	30,424 tons (27,600 tonnes)
ANNUAL CONSUMPTION PER PERSON: 2 lb. 14 oz. (1.3 kg)	

uncommon to find an estate just a few miles from the beach, bordered by tropical jungle, and often part of a larger plantation that might also produce other crops such as cinnamon, rubber and coconuts.

Sri Lanka produces tea all year round but the country does have distinct dry and rainy seasons, with two monsoon seasons setting in during the year: the south-western monsoon between May and September, and the northeastern monsoon between October and January.

The most sought-after, premium teas tend to be produced from slower-growing plants in the hill country where the mountains provide shelter, letting just enough rain and wind through to create the perfect microclimate.

Plantations in the tropical, low-country areas produce the biggest yields because of the sunnier conditions and moisture throughout the year. This means that the tea shrubs grow taller and faster, develop more polyphenols (from the sunshine) and are generally sturdier. This makes the teas produced here stronger in taste, but without as much depth of flavor.

The tea industry in Sri Lanka is still very much based upon the traditional hand-plucking and processing methods, as used since the plantations were established in the 19th century. Although machinery is advancing and some factories are lucky enough to be able to implement new technology, the majority of plantations don't have the finances to upgrade their machinery.

TEAS

Sri Lanka produces mostly orthodox black teas but also produces CTC, white and green teas. Over the last 10 years green tea production has grown, with three factories having converted from black to green tea production.

The two types of green tea produced are the gunpowder type, prepared using the Chinese method of drying the leaves, and sencha, using the Japanese method of steaming the leaves (see page 212). The former is strong in taste while the latter is delicate.

Opposite: Tea pickers, like these Tamil women, must have the leaves they pick checked for quality, weighed and recorded at intervals throughout the day.
Right: Each week, the biggest tea auction in the world is held in Sri Lanka's commercial capital, Colombo.

COLOMBO TEA AUCTIONS

In a system unique to Sri Lanka, all tea produced in the country must be sent to government-regulated tea auctions, held every week in Colombo, to be graded, tasted, priced and sold. There are also smaller numbers of prearranged sales, but these must always be cleared by the Tea Board before any contract can be agreed.

Every week, prior to the auctions, samples from all the teas produced are sent around the registered list of tea buyers in the country. Each of these buyers will taste and grade the teas, making note of any of interest. Each company then sends a team of buyers to the auctions, who act on behalf of their clients. There are also brokers present to represent each tea estate. Then follows the balancing act between the brokers, who are there to get the best price for the estates, and the buyers, who want to get the best price for their customers.

Even if they do not plan to buy any tea in a particular week, members of the buying companies still attend the auctions to record sale prices and to keep abreast of trends. The tea market is treated very much like the stock market: it has to be monitored and reviewed to keep on top of price fluctuations and changes in demand. A variety of factors, such as the weather, political events and public holidays, can affect a batch's price — and auctioneers, brokers and buyers all know that the real money in tea is made and lost at auction.

Over 30 percent of Sri Lanka's tea crop is grown in regions that are classified as "high country," like this plantation in the Matale area of Kandy, in the center of the island.

REGIONS

UVA (HIGH GROWN)

Tea type: Aromatic black tea perfect for English breakfast blends

Climate/terrain: 3,280 to 5,250 ft. (1,000–1,600 m); monsoon blows through passes; mostly dry, hot days, cool nights

Location: Eastern slopes of Sri Lanka's central hill country

Estates/plantations: Halpewatte, Greenland, Adawatte

KANDY (HIGH GROWN)

Tea type: Black tea that is stronger, full-bodied and with a deeper-colored liquor

Climate/terrain: 2,135 to 4,625 ft. (650–1,300 m); sheltered mountainside terrain and stable, cool, dry weather except during monsoon

Location: Center of hill country

Estates/plantations: Geragama, Ashburnham

NUWARA ELIYA (HIGH GROWN)

Tea type: High-quality black teas, light in taste and delicately fragrant aroma

Climate/terrain: 6,560 ft. (2,000 m); high mountains; cool air and steady rainfall, fragrant mists

Location: Center of hill country

Estates/plantations: Mackwoods, Pedro, Lover's Leap

UDA PUSSELLAWA (MID-GROWN)

Tea type: Black tea with medium body and tangy taste

Climate/terrain: 3,115 to 3,250 ft. (950–1,600 m); two "quality seasons" like its neighbors Uva and Nuwara Eliya; mostly wet and misty thought the year

Location: Center of hill country

Estates/plantations: Finlays

THE CHAMPAGNE REGION

The dry season in the hill country region of Nuwara Eliya, which runs between May and August, is world renowned for the quality of the tea produced. This has gained the area the nickname "the Champagne region."

Sea air blows through the mountains, creating a fragrance and aroma that cannot be replicated anywhere else or at any other time of year. Still today, the factories atop the hilly estates will use just the fresh sea air to wither their leaves.

Right: An overseer weighs a basket of broken orange pekoe leaves at a plantation in the Nuwara Eliya region.

DIMBULA (HIGH GROWN)

Tea type: Bright, rich black tea with strong, refreshing flavor

Climate/terrain: 4,920 to 5,900 ft. (1,500–1,800 m); valley, therefore wet and misty for most of the year; cool spring breezes bring fragrances, such as jasmine and cypress, to the leaves

Location: Central but to the east of the hill country

Estates/plantations: Bogahawatte, Kirkoswald

RUHUNA (LOW GROWN)

Tea type: Robust, strong black teas; good with milk

Climate/terrain: Varies dramatically with coastline, hills inland and even some tropical rainforests

Location: Southern coast and tip of the island

Estates/plantations: Lumbini

PO CHA (YAK BUTTER TEA)

Yak butter tea, or po cha, is a warming, high-calorie tea made from boiled tea, yak butter and salt. It is a staple of the Himalayan diet, playing a key role in the health, hospitality and status of the people who live surrounded by the highest mountains in the world. Po cha's flavor and aroma are often described as thick, oily, buttery, earthy and pungent.

TEA LEAF OF CHOICE

Po cha is made from black or pu'erh tea, traditionally in brick form, which is the most suitable for transporting and storing in these remote mountain regions. The rocky, high-altitude terrain makes it impossible to cultivate tea plantations, so all the tea consumed in the Himalayas is grown in lower-lying provinces of China.

HOW IS IT MADE AND SERVED

Po cha is made by boiling tea leaves for up to half a day to create a dark-brown, almost black, tea concentrate that can then be stored for a further 3 days. As needed, the concentrate is heated and added to a tall, cylindrical wooden churn where it is mixed with yak butter and salt.

Wealthy Himalayan families will serve po cha in ornate gold, silver and jade teacups that have been passed down through the generations. The po cha teacup is a symbol of status and even the most basic wooden teacups will be lined with silver and jewels, and people carry them on their person wherever they go.

SOCIETY AND CULTURE

Po cha developed out of the necessity for a high intake of fat and salt to help maintain warmth and energy levels, crucial when living a nomadic life in high altitudes and surviving in some of the world's most challenging terrain.

It also plays a big part in hospitality — all guests invited into a home in Lhasa receive a cup of po cha and their cup will never be allowed to become empty.

HISTORY

During the ninth century the Chinese Empire sought to expand its number of horses and the inhabitants of Lhasa were rapidly developing an obsession with tea, so the Tea Horse Route was born (see page 65). The pu'erh tea brick holds some of its origins in this trade route, too. Not only was it the easiest way to transport and preserve the tea leaves for their year-long journey across the mountains, but it was also used as currency.

Opposite, above: Herdsmen in the Himalayas rely on yak butter tea to supply much-needed calories and warmth at high altitudes.

Opposite, below: A young monk pours yak butter tea, which is consumed in countries throughout the Himalayas.

THE
MIDDLE
EAST

Some of the world's most dedicated tea lovers are found in the Middle East, as well as two of the world's leading tea producers — Turkey and Iran. Tea in Turkey is consumed at the highest rate in the world, Turkish people each enjoying, on average, over 10 cups a day. Tea is also drunk in Egypt, Morocco and Georgia, although only commercially produced in Georgia.

TEA-PRODUCING COUNTRIES

(IN ORDER OF PRODUCTION VOLUME)

TURKEY

All of Turkey's tea is grown around the Rize region, which is the only part of the country that has the climate just right for producing tea. Although this may sound restrictive, Turkey produces a high yield each year and most of it serves the domestic market.

Produces: 234,130 tons (212,400 tonnes)
Exports: 3,860 tons (3,500 tonnes)
Imports: 5,620 tons (5,100 tonnes)
Consumes: 221,015 tons (200,500 tonnes)
Annual consumption per person: 4 lb. 10 oz. (2.1 kg)
Tea profile: Black teas and some green teas also

IRAN

The Iranian people consume a vast amount of tea and the country's tea industry mostly produces just to serve the domestic market.

Produces: 176,370 tons (160,000 tonnes)
Exports: 12,355 tons (11,210 tonnes)
Imports: 70,080 tons (63,555 tonnes)
Consumes: 151,990 tons (137,885 tonnes)
Annual consumption per person: 4 lb. 1 oz. (1.83 kg)
Tea profile: Light black teas

GEORGIA

Twenty years ago tea was a large part of the Georgian economy but rapid expansion saw quality drop and the industry falter. Today, a few dedicated Georgian estates are helping revive the industry by going back to basics and producing good-quality teas.

Produces: 3,640 tons (3,300 tonnes)
Exports: 2,535 tons (2,300 tonnes)
Imports: 2,095 tons (1,900 tonnes)
Consumes: 3,750 tons (3,400 tonnes)
Annual consumption per person: 12 oz. (330 g)
Tea profile: Strong, fragrant black teas, great with milk

Previous pages: Turkey's Rize region, situated on the Black Sea, has two main agricultural products: tea and kiwi fruit.

Opposite, above: Tea was first grown in Georgia around 1830. Although the local tea industry has now rather fallen into decline, recently the state has set aside funds to help restore Georgia's tea plantations.

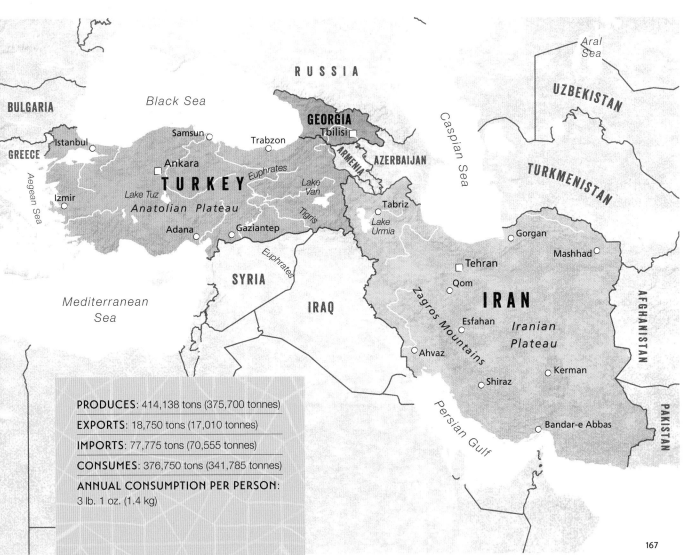

PRODUCES: 414,138 tons (375,700 tonnes)

EXPORTS: 18,750 tons (17,010 tonnes)

IMPORTS: 77,775 tons (70,555 tonnes)

CONSUMES: 376,750 tons (341,785 tonnes)

ANNUAL CONSUMPTION PER PERSON:
3 lb. 1 oz. (1.4 kg)

TURKEY

Although still fairly new to growing tea, Turkey is already a major world player both in terms of tea production and tea consumption. Production levels have risen rapidly over the last century, all in the Rize region, to place Turkey fifth on the list of tea producers worldwide. In terms of tea consumed per country, Turkey is fourth in the world, which is quite an achievement in itself. However, when it comes to tea consumed per person, Turkish people are the world's biggest tea drinkers. Almost all the tea the country produces is destined for the domestic market. Turkey's black teas, which are served sweet and black in small glass cups placed on a porcelain or metal saucer, are ingrained in social customs surrounding hospitality,

Above: The climate created by the combination of sea and mountains make the Rize area the only place in Turkey suitable for cultivating tea.

PRODUCES: 234,130 tons (212,400 tonnes)

EXPORTS: 3,860 tons (3,500 tonnes)

IMPORTS: 5,620 tons (5,100 tonnes)

CONSUMES: 221,015 tons (200,500 tonnes)

ANNUAL CONSUMPTION PER PERSON:
4 lb. 10 oz. (2.1 kg)

friendship and commerce. Tea, or *cay*, is enjoyed everywhere, from roadside tea stands to high-class social occasions, and by people from all walks of life.

HISTORY AND DEVELOPMENT

Japanese tea plants were first planted in Turkey in the late 1800s, but cultivation did not take off on a larger scale at the time. For the next century, the Turkish government continued to take small steps toward larger-scale tea production in various forms, but numerous initiatives and organizations failed to make any serious headway. It was not until the 1930s that three important factors combined to really kick-start Turkey's tea production: first, the establishment of a research team that examined the potential and challenged the existing methods of

tea production in Turkey; second, the introduction of a government guarantee to purchase any unsold tea; and, third, an influx of immigrants following World War I, who were incentivized to set up farms.

It is perhaps these efforts by the government to push domestic purchase and consumption of tea, combined with a drop in imports during World War II, that fueled the rapid growth of tea cultivation in Turkey, almost wholly for the domestic market. By the 1960s Turkey's tea industry had grown so large that it was able to meet domestic demand and the government took various steps to protect its own interests by placing a higher tax on tea imports than any other tea-producing country. The government also controls the ports through which it is imported but a large amount is still smuggled in illegally.

Today, the government owns 60 percent of the tea industry in the form of around 50 factories and processing facilities, under the organization of the state tea company, Çaykur, with the remainder owned by private farmers and companies. The Turkish government has been trying to make the tea industry sufficiently large to support the setting up of numerous export brands, but, as yet, this hasn't been achieved to the desired levels. Turkey faced a setback following the Chernobyl disaster, in what is now Ukraine, in 1986, when all Turkish tea exports were halted because some tea plants tested high in radioactive contaminants following radioactive rainfall in the region.

However, it has since recovered. Turkey's biggest export markets are the European Union, India, Russia and the United States.

CLIMATE, TERRAIN AND HARVESTING

All Turkish tea is produced in a small area surrounding the city of Rize, situated on Turkey's northeast coast, on the Black Sea. This is because the typical Turkish climate is not suitable for cultivating tea; it is only because of a unique set of conditions that tea can grow in this region. Rize has a gentle climate and its coastal location, combined with shelter inland provided by the Kaçkar Mountains, traps in the moist sea air, ensuring plenty of rainfall and nutrient-rich soil.

The weather tends to be wet between September and January, and the main harvest takes place between May and October. It is usual to get three harvests a year but the weather can at times be unpredictably cold and rainy, causing frost and landslides. When unexpected frost hits, it is difficult to get all three harvests in the dry season, while landslides can wipe out whole tea fields. This can cost the producers dearly and has a major impact on the nation's economy.

Below: From business meetings to weddings, there is no facet of Turkish life in which tea — served in a tulip-shaped glass and diluted to taste with boiling water — does not have a role.

REGIONS

Sixty-six percent of Turkish tea is grown around Rize itself, with the rest grown in the wider Rize region. Twenty percent is grown in Trabzon, 11 percent in Artvin and 3 percent in Giresun/Ordu. Although grown in different provinces, the following statistics for the Rize region are applicable to all Turkish teas because it is grown along a small strip of coastline.

RIZE REGION
Tea type: Black tea
Climate/terrain: Coastal, low altitude, sheltered by mountain range; wet with nutrient-rich soil
Location: Turkey's northeast coast, on the Black Sea
Plantations: Rize, Trabzon, Artvin, Giresun and Ordu

TYPES OF TEA GROWN IN TURKEY

Turkey produces mostly black teas, with a small amount of green tea production set up in 2003. The government is trying to push the production of higher-quality, and more varied single-estate teas for the export market but, as domestic demand is so high, this isn't taking off on a big scale. The domestic preparation of tea — the locals drink it very strong and over-steeped — means that there is no call for variation in production or tea type. Therefore, it is rare to find any specifics about teas produced in Turkey, as they are all grown under roughly the same conditions and mostly processed by the centrally owned Çaykur factories.

Tea farmers preparing their produce for sale in the hills of Rize, on Turkey's Black Sea coast. For centuries, coffee was a key element in the Ottoman way of life, but today the people of Turkey drink more tea per person than anyone else in the world.

TURKISH RIZE TEA AND THE ÇAYDANLIK TEAPOT

There is hardly a situation or time of day that isn't considered suitable for tea in Turkey — it is a truly versatile drink, enjoyed across all levels of society, and plays a huge role in demonstrating hospitality and friendship.

Tea is usually taken black and sweet. Turkish people have a unique method of serving tea, first pouring a shot of strong, concentrated tea into a glass, and then diluting it with boiling water to their preferred strength.

HOW IS IT MADE AND SERVED

Turkish tea has its own unique tools and serving methods that are famous the world over. Only one type of tea is produced in Turkey, Rize black tea, which is served strong, with sugar, in a small glass that can get hot enough to burn your fingers.

The first unique factor about Turkish tea-making is the use of a çaydanlık, a type of Turkish samovar — a hot-water kettle topped with a teapot, both of which are traditionally made of metal. The samovar itself isn't native to Turkey, but borrowed from Russia (where people also appreciate their tea very strong and black).

The upper pot, containing tea leaves, is placed on top of the water-filled lower pot and put onto the stove to boil. Once the water has come to the boil, half of the water is poured into the upper pot, then the pots are stacked on one above the other again and returned to the heat. This allows the leaves to begin infusing in the upper pot, with the steam rising from the lower pot keeping the water hot enough to stew the leaves for at least 20 minutes — creating the famous strength of flavor of Turkish tea.

The strong, concentrated tea is poured into glass cups, filling them about halfway, and boiling water from the lower pot is used to dilute the tea to the drinker's desired strength. In Turkey, you will often hear people say *koyu* — dark and strong — or *açık* — light and weak — as every Turk knows how they like their tea. The tea drinkers will usually add their preferred amount of sugar at this stage also. The pots are then placed back onto the stove to remain warm for further servings.

TURKISH APPLE TEA

Most visitors to Turkey will come away with fond memories of an apple-flavored tea served to them by welcoming Turks throughout their travels. The custom of serving apple-flavored tea to tourists is widespread, goes down well and has, unsurprisingly, led to the belief that the national tea-based drink of Turkey is apple tea. However, this isn't the case.

The myth of Turkish apple tea probably comes from a combination of Turkey's abundance of flavored and herbal teas and the social importance of tea in hospitality and commerce. For example, tea is almost always served at business meetings or to customers in shops (to keep you there longer and to literally sweeten the deal). So Turkish tea was served to tourists in shops, cafés and hotels as a gesture of welcome, but it soon become apparent that traditional Turkish tea was much too strong and not very palatable to visitors. Flavored teas started to be offered instead, with apple becoming the most popular over time. This has led to myriad companies, both in Turkey and in other countries, producing flavored black teas and labeling them "Turkish Apple Tea" in an attempt to cash in on the drink's popularity. It is common for these blends of tea to be made with purely artificial apple flavoring, without any actual apple — and, in some cases, not even any tea.

Opposite: Typically, Turkish tea is made in a *çaydanlık*, which is a metal kettle with a smaller metal teapot stacked on top of it.

IRAN

Tea production was first introduced to Iran by Prince Mohammad Mirza, who served as Iran's ambassador to India. In the 1890s he smuggled Indian tea saplings out of India and then planted them in his home town of Lahijan (see the box on page 178 for more on this). Factories and further plantations were quick to follow.

Iran may be relatively new to tea production, but the country has a long-standing tea-drinking culture, as well as a good climate and terrain that have the potential to support an important production industry. On the surface this already seems to be the case, as Iran has tripled its production over the last 10 years to establish itself as the seventh largest producer in the world. However, cracks are beginning to show in the Iranian tea industry as demand falls because of large-scale importing of tea produced outside of Iran. This has seen many of those originally made rich through tea cultivation abandon the industry for other trades, such as farming or property investment.

HISTORY AND DEVELOPMENT

Tea has been enjoyed widely in Iran since ancient trade routes brought goods from China to the West. By the end of the 19th century local consumption was more than large enough to support its own tea production and Prince Mohammad Mirza was the one who set about making it happen.

Iran built its first tea factory in the 1930s and the industry has since grown to span over 100 factories and 86,500 acres (35,000 hectares) of tea farms. The initial investment has paid off, as demonstrated by the thousands of tons of tea Iran produces each year. However, consumption levels of domestic, unbranded Iranian tea are declining, in favor of more fashionable, branded teas produced elsewhere so, without an

PRODUCES: 176,370 tons (160,000 tonnes)

EXPORTS: 12,355 tons (11,210 tonnes)

IMPORTS: 70,0820 tons (63,555 tonnes)

CONSUMES: 151,990 tons (137,885 tonnes)

ANNUAL CONSUMPTION PER PERSON:
4 lb. (1.83 kg)

Above: A teahouse, or *chaikaneh*, in Isfahan, a city in western Iran long known as the Florence of Persia due to its beautiful 17th-century architecture. Once the province of men only, teahouses are now frequented by all members of Iranian society.

adequate export market, supply threatens to outstrip demand. Illegal trading of these teas has proved to be a large obstacle to the growth of Iran's domestic tea industry. The government has attempted to control tea imports — both legal and illegal — with varied levels of effort and success. The impact on the Iranian tea industry has been great, with many factories sitting empty or running at half capacity and many farmers and workers left with fields full of tea and no income.

With a growth in demand for high-quality branded teas, especially among the upper classes of Iran, the ability to really focus on and produce teas to meet this domestic market, increase exports and control the illegal trading of tea, is going to make or break the industry over the next few years.

CLIMATE, TERRAIN AND HARVESTING

Iran's teas are cultivated in the hills of the province of Gilan, which lies just below the Caspian Sea. The combination of the hilly terrain and coastal weather means that the area is humid and lush with regular rainfall — making it perfect for tea production.

THE IRANIAN PRINCE OF TEA

An Iranian ambassador to India during the time the subcontinent was under British rule, Prince Mirza had plenty of access to the Indian tea industry. He knew how much people in his own country loved to drink tea and that the climate in his home town of Lahijan would be perfect for tea cultivation.

However, the Prince also knew that the British kept their Indian tea industry under close guard and that they would never agree to him using the plants or skills cultivated there to set up a rival industry in Iran. So he adopted the disguise of a French laborer to get a job on a plantation to learn the ropes and, ultimately, to smuggle tea saplings back into Iran.

His political immunity meant that the British couldn't search his belongings or question him upon re-entry into Iran and so he succeeded in his plans. In the end he smuggled thousands of saplings into Iran and planted them in the northern province of Gilan. The rest is history.

REGIONS

Apart for the occasional small farm, Iran's teas are all grown around the town of Lahijan, Gilan province. The towns and villages in Lahijan sit just back from the Caspian seafront, with tea plantations dotted south of the city on the misty hillsides.

LAHIJAN COUNTY

Tea type: Black orthodox tea
Climate/terrain: Coastal, hillside terrain with regular moist and misty weather
Location: Iran's north coast, on the Caspian Sea
Plantations: Various family-owned farms and factories, all in the Lahijan area

TYPES OF TEA GROWN IN IRAN

Almost all Iranian tea is black orthodox tea for the domestic, unbranded market. It is therefore unusual to find an Iranian tea outside Iran, especially one with a particular name or flavor profile. The few available to purchase outside of Iran are simply called "Gilan tea."

Iranian black teas all have a light flavor and a red tone to their liquor. The Lahijan hillside terrain is not too dissimilar to the Darjeeling region of India (see page 150) so light, fragrant flavors, often found in Darjeeling teas, can be present, although this is not common. Iranian teas also go well without milk, are often taken with the addition of sugar and can be brewed in a samovar (see 174).

Iran also grows a small amount of green tea, which is also taken sweet.

Left: With its mild climate, Gilan Province is well suited to growing tea. Originally established by Prince Mohammad Mirza in the 1890s, tea cultivation quickly expanded in the region.

FAR EAST

Home to a vast variety of tea types, customs and traditions, the Far East is the most influential region in the world when it comes to tea. The consumption levels of tea in the Far East are almost double those of the next largest consumers in the Indian subcontinent. The Indian subcontinent exports more tea than the Far East but the production and consumption levels highlight the different approach to tea the two areas have: in India and Sri Lanka, tea may be a booming export industry, but in China and Japan it is a way of life. Most of the teas produced in the Far East are still green teas made using traditional methods of steaming and pan-firing (see page 57), as well as delicately scented white and oolong teas. China is home to the largest tea-drinking population on the planet and, although it is by far the world's largest producer of tea, a large percentage of its production is consumed by the domestic market.

TEA-PRODUCING COUNTRIES

(IN ORDER OF PRODUCTION VOLUME)

CHINA, MAINLAND

The true home of tea, China has about 5,000 years on the rest of the world both in terms of tea drinking and cultivation. The variety of teas produced by China is mind-blowing and it would take a connoisseur a lifetime to explore all of them. Most of the tea produced here is green and consumed by the local market, but China still manages to export over 350,000 tons (almost 320,000 tonnes) around the world.

Produces: 2,121,350 tons (1,924,455 tonnes)
Exports: 352,000 tons (319,360 tonnes)
Imports: 67,670 tons (61,415 tonnes)
Consumes: 1,777,245 tons (1,612,290 tonnes)
Annual consumption per person: 2 lb. 7 oz. (1.1 kg)
Tea profile: Wide variety of green teas; black, pu'erh, oolong and white teas, too

TAIWAN, CHINA

Taiwan has contributed so much to the tea industry in terms of new production methods and tea varieties. The island produces some of the best oolongs in the world, including a unique type of oolong, pouchong, created in Pinglin. Taiwan is also the birthplace of the iconic "bubble tea" — sweet milky tea, usually shaken with fruit syrups and tapioca pearls.

Produces: 16,425 tons (14,900 tonnes)
Exports: 3,465 tons (3,145 tonnes)
Imports: 32,960 tons (29,900 tonnes)
Consumes: 45,195 tons (41,000 tonnes)
Annual consumption per person: 3 lb. 12 oz. (1.7 kg)
Tea profile: Oolong teas; some pu'erh, black and green teas also

Previous pages: Neat rows of tea bushes in the mountainous Moc Chau district of Vietnam, which lies about 125 mi. (200 km) northwest of Hanoi.

KAZAKHSTAN

RUSSIA

MONGOLIA

Tien Shan

Takla Makan
Desert

CHINA

NORTH
KOREA

Sea of
Japan

Beijing ☐
Tianjin ○

Huang He

SOUTH
KOREA

JAPAN

Tokyo ☐

Yellow
Sea

Plateau
of Tibet

Yangtze

Mekong

Salween

Xi'an ○

Great Plain
of China

Chengdu ○

Yangtze

Wuhan ○

Shanghai ○

Himalaya

Brahmaputra

Chongqing ○

Hangzhou ○

East
China
Sea

NEPAL

BHUTAN

Ganges

INDIA

Irrawaddy

Xi Jiang

Guangzhou ○

Shantou ○

Taipei ○
Taiwan

PACIFIC
OCEAN

BURMA
(MYANMAR)

Hanoi ☐

Hong Kong ○

Bay of
Bengal

LAOS

VIETNAM

South
China
Sea

Philippine
Sea

THAILAND

Bangkok ☐

CAMBODIA

PHILIPPINES

INDIAN
OCEAN

Gulf of Thailand

Ho Chi Minh City ○

BRUNEI

Celebes
Sea

Kuala Lumpur ☐ MALAYSIA

0   miles   1000

0   km   1000

SINGAPORE

INDONESIA

PAPUA
NEW
GUINEA

Jakarta ☐

Java Sea

EAST
TIMOR

AUSTRALIA

PRODUCES: 2,733,730 tons (2,480,000 tonnes)

EXPORTS: 600,760 tons (545,000 tonnes)

IMPORTS: 181,565 tons (164,715 tonnes)

ANNUAL CONSUMPTION PER PERSON:
2 lb. 10 oz. (1.2 kg)

VIETNAM

Vietnam has excellent conditions for growing tea but the industry has been rocked over the years by the country's unstable economy. Teas are produced for both export and domestic markets. Vietnam is particularly famous for its scented teas.

Produces: 236,225 tons (214,300 tonnes)
Exports: 161,710 tons (146,700 tonnes)
Imports: 220 tons (200 tonnes)
Consumes: 79,335 tons (72,000 tonnes)
Annual consumption per person: 1 lb. 8 oz. (700 g)
Tea profile: Black CTC teas, high-mountain oolongs and scented teas

INDONESIA

The tea grown on Java, particularly in the west of the island, is said to be of the highest quality in Indonesia, although tea is also grown on two of the nation's smaller islands: Sumatra and Sulawesi. The black teas produced are often compared favorably to Sri Lankan teas because of their light fragrance.

Produces: 163,140 tons (148,000 tonnes)
Exports: 77,240 tons (70,070 tonnes)
Imports: 26,895 tons (24,395 tonnes)
Consumes: 104,435 tons (94,740 tonnes)
Annual consumption per person: 13 oz. (380 g)
Tea profile: Light black teas with unique, delicate fragrance

JAPAN

Although Japan is smaller in terms of production than some other countries in the region, its tea culture is possibly the most famous in the world. Tea is such an ingrained part of Japanese society and customs that the country has to import 44,090 tons (40,000 tonnes) a year, on top of the 93,475 tons (84,800 tonnes) it produces itself, just to meet local demand. Japan also produces matcha (see page 218), a powdered green tea particularly enjoyed for its health benefits and celebrated as part of the traditional Buddhist tea ceremony.

Produces: 93,475 tons (84,800 tonnes)
Exports: 2,755 tons (2,500 tonnes)
Imports: 44,090 tons (40,000 tonnes)
Consumes: 136,025 tons (123,400 tonnes)
Annual consumption per person: 3 lb. 5 oz. (1.5 kg)
Tea profile: Wide variety of green teas, including matcha, with some black and white also

THAILAND

Tea is produced mainly in Thailand's northern region, in the same type of forested land found in tea-producing areas of Yunnan in China and Assam in India. Thai teas are mostly oolong and green, although some traditional pu'erh is still produced by the Shan people (see page 222). Thai teas have a good reputation in terms of quality, although they are often hard to find outside of the country itself.

Produces: 82,675 tons (75,000 tonnes)
Exports: 1,655 tons (1,500 tonnes)
Imports: 6,175 tons (5,600 tonnes)
Consumes: 85,980 tons (78,000 tonnes)
Annual consumption per person: 2 lb. 7 oz. (1.1 kg)
Tea profile: Green, oolong, black and pu'erh teas

MALAYSIA

The Cameron Highlands in Malaysia perhaps have the most accessible tea plantations in the world, opening their doors to tourists and visitors all year round. The teas produced are mostly orthodox black grades that are good quality but tend to be lighter than others produced in the area.

Produces: 70,550 tons (64,000 tonnes)
Exports: 2,205 tons (2,000 tonnes)
Imports: 20,060 tons (18,200 tonnes)
Consumes: 36,375 tons (33,000 tonnes)
Annual consumption per person: 3 lb. 1 oz. (1.4 kg)
Tea profile: Light, fragrant black teas, with some green

Left: Vietnamese farmers expertly balance their baskets loaded with freshly picked tea leaves. In Vietnam, tea is typically harvested three to four times a year.

CHINA

Home of the very first tea plants, with an ancient tea-drinking culture that goes back thousands of years, China has influenced tea production and cultivation all over the globe for centuries.

Today China is the world's largest tea producer by a long way and its tea industry continues to grow at a rapid rate, matched by no other country in the world. Take into consideration that China produces the widest variety of tea in the world and that the Chinese consume the second largest amount of tea per person per year, and it is fair to say that China sits at the center of the modern world of tea.

Above: Morning mist hangs over a high-altitude tea plantation in Zhejiang, a coastal province in southeastern China. Dragon Well, green and gunpowder green teas are grown in Zhejiang, China's leading province for tea production.

HISTORY AND DEVELOPMENT

In 2004, scientists excavating at the foot of Tianluo Hill in the north of Zhejiang Province discovered ancient tea-plant fossils with marks indicating cultivation. These findings have shaken up all prior beliefs about the age of the tea industry. Previously, the earliest recorded example of tea, which was also found in China, dated back to 3000 BCE. These remarkable new findings place the new date for the origin of tea cultivation at nearly 9,000 years ago.

The earliest written record of tea is from China and dates back to 600 BCE. The first known book about brewing and serving tea, written by the Chinese poet Lu Yu, followed shortly after (see page 61). For much of Chinese history, tea has been hailed for its role in both herbal medicine and ceremony.

PRODUCES: 2,121,350 tons (1,924,455 tonnes)

EXPORTS: 352,030 tons (319,355 tonnes)

IMPORTS: 67,670 tons (61,415 tonnes)

CONSUMES: 1,777,246 tons (1,612,290 tonnes)

ANNUAL CONSUMPTION PER PERSON:
2 lb. 7 oz. (1.1 kg)

Traditional methods of plucking, pan-drying and rolling tea leaves, all done by hand, are still practiced in many areas of China, producing some of the most sought-after teas in the world. However, many companies have

CHINESE WOMAN GATHERING TEA.—FROM A DRAWING BY A CHINESE ARTIST.

established mass-scale processing facilities, where most of production is now mechanical.

The majority of Chinese tea is green or oolong, with some traditional production of pu'erh and a more recent focus on black teas for export such as Keemun, Yunnan and lapsang souchong.

CLIMATE, TERRAIN AND HARVESTING

There is a vast variety of Chinese teas, grown under an equally wide variety of climate conditions and in many types of terrain. The tea leaves are harvested at different times throughout the year — usually spring, summer and autumn — but not usually during the winter as temperatures are too low.

The first spring harvest is considered the highest quality and makes up nearly half of all production. In some of China's most southern provinces, such as Yunnan, the climate is warm and sunny enough for the first harvest to

be as early as February, but in the cooler northern regions the plants might not be ready until May.

Some of the most interesting and sought-after flavors of tea originate from the mountain regions of China, where a few unique climate and terrain factors combine to make the teas very special. First, the high elevation means that cool air circulates around the peaks of the mountains. Second, the mountains provide shelter from the monsoons while still ensuring lots of mist and rainfall. Finally, the winds and the monsoons bring in various aromas that are infused into the leaves.

Chinese teas have been harvested and processed by hand for thousands of years. Chinese processing methods in particular have guided and shaped production in many other countries, as well as serving as a benchmark when creating machinery to take over from people. Tea-processing machines were developed to replicate the touch and heat that were painstakingly applied by hand, thereby more than doubling processing speed and halving labor costs. These machines are more efficient for sure, but there is some argument as to whether they can produce a superior tea, so many high-quality teas are still processed by hand.

Nearly all Chinese teas are still picked by hand. With the majority of tea types, the pickers aim to pluck the top two leaves and the bud of the plant. There are a few exceptions in China, particularly with oolong, where it's possible to harvest a few of the lower leaves along with the top two and the bud, and also with lapsang souchong, for which the lower, darker and harder leaves are required.

"NOT FOR ALL THE TEA IN CHINA"

This saying was coined around the turn of the 19th century, probably in Australia, and refers to the large amount of tea that China is known to produce. The phrase is used to demonstrate a determination not to do something: "No way, not at any cost — not for all the tea in China."

Opposite: Painted on silk, this is an early 18th-century depiction of farmers in China sorting tea leaves for transportation.

REGIONS

Tea is produced in nearly 20 regions across China, but the main ones are:

FUJIAN

Tea type: White silver needle, Wuyi Mountain oolong tea, tie guan yin, black guyi teas, lapsang souchong

Climate/terrain: High-altitude, misty, very mountainous terrain; subtropical climate with wet/dry seasons but some rainfall all year

Location: Southeast coast of China

Tea gardens/farm locations: Wuyi, Funding, Anxi

YUNNAN

Tea type: Green Yunnan, pu'erh Yunnan

Climate/terrain: Forested, mountainous terrain; seasonal monsoon weather — heavy rainfall, warm climate, excellent irrigation from the Mekong River

Location: Southwest China, bordering Tibet, Vietnam, Laos and Myanmar

Tea gardens/farm locations: Puer, Lincang, Baoshan, Xishuangbanna

ZHEJIANG

Tea type: Dragon Well (lung ching) green tea, gunpowder green tea

Climate/terrain: Mountainous terrain, some high-altitude farms; subtropical, humid, plenty of rainfall but clear seasonal weather pattern

Location: East coast of China

Tea gardens/farm locations: Hangzhou, Pingshui, Anji

JIANGXI

Tea type: Dongding, Keemun, chun mee

Climate/terrain: Mountainous, high altitude; subtropical, humid, dry in winter, very wet in summer

Location: Landlocked province in southeastern China

Tea gardens/farm locations: Suzhou, Wuyuan

ANHUI

Tea type: Keemun, mao feng, chun mee

Climate/terrain: Variable climate and terrain

Location: East China

Tea gardens/farm locations: Qimen, Jinzhai, Huangshan

TYPES OF TEA GROWN IN CHINA

China produces almost all types of tea and many varieties of each type. The majority of tea produced here is green and destined for the huge domestic market, with a wider variety — but much smaller quantities — of black and oolongs being produced for export. China mainly exports its tea to its neighboring Asian countries, as well as to Russia and Europe.

The names of Chinese teas can be confusing, as there are often a few different pronunciations and spellings, as well as nicknames for teas based upon their appearance or on a legend. Unlike the teas of other countries, which are named after the area in which they are grown, Chinese teas are a little more complicated. It is common for there to be various types of each named tea, such as a green Yunnan and a black Yunnan tea, for example, or a black Keemun, a Keemun mao feng and a mao feng green.

TIE GUAN YIN (iron goddess of mercy, iron Buddha)

Region: Anxi, Fujian Province

Climate/terrain: Mountain-grown in misty climate

Processing methods: Roasted by traditional Chinese methods and semi-oxidized

Taste profile: Depending on dark or light roast — toasted, sweet and complex

DRAGON WELL (lung ching, long jing)

Region: Hangzhou, Zhejiang Province

Climate/terrain: Mountain-grown in misty climate

Processing methods: Pan-fired to create very flat, long leaves

Taste profile: Rich, gem-green liquor, mellow flavor with sweet, grassy aftertaste. No bitterness.

CHUN MEE (zhen mei, precious eyebrows)

Region: Jiangxi Province, Zhejiang Province, Anhui Province

Climate/terrain: High elevation — 3,280 ft. (1,000 m), mountainous terrain; subtropical and humid

Processing methods: Pan-fired, hand-rolled into "eyebrow" shape

Taste profile: Brisk and often smoky, not sweet but smooth on the palate

MAO FENG

Region: Anhui Province

Climate/terrain: Grown near the Huangshan mountain range; clouded and humid all year; harvested in early spring for best flavors

Processing methods: Dependent on type of mao feng — all are naturally dried to preserve fine hairs, or fur, on the leaves (*mao feng* means "fur peak")

Taste profile: Light, delicate fruit aromas and clean grassy flavors, clear pale-green liquor

LAPSANG SOUCHONG

Region: Fujian Province

Climate/terrain: High altitude in Wuyi Mountains, very steep, rough terrain; subtropical climate with wet/dry seasonality

Processing methods: Larger leaves harvested, dried over pine fires, then black tea processing

Taste profile: Smoked aroma, smoky flavor with smooth mouthfeel and distinct aftertaste

KEEMUN

Region: Anhui Province

Climate/terrain: Depends on type of Keemun

Processing methods: Slow withering and oxidization compared to other black teas

Taste profile: Distinct aromatic flavors with floral notes and sometimes sweet

Opposite: A UNESCO World Heritage Site, the Wuyi Mountains in Fujian Province produce a variety of teas, including oolong and lapsang souchong.

Deep-red autumn leaves
punctuate the serried rows
of dark-green tea bushes at this
Chinese plantation.

TAIWAN, CHINA

The island of Taiwan is significant in the world of tea because of the number of unique teas that have been developed there. The majority of Taiwan's low-altitude coastal plains are not "usual" for top-quality tea cultivation but, combined with the high-altitude misty mountain range running down the island's center, it adds an interesting element to tea production. It is because of this that Taiwan produces some of the world's best oolong teas, including pouchong, created in and around Pinglin village, which is a lighter, almost green tea, with floral notes. Taiwan is responsible for nearly 20 percent of the world's production of oolong as well as producing black, green and white teas. Teas from Taiwan are commonly labeled "Formosa" after the historical name of the island.

Above: Taiwan has two distinct tea-growing terrains: low-altitude plains and mist-shrouded mountain ranges.

HISTORY AND DEVELOPMENT

In the 1800s, when the black tea industry was booming in Ceylon (now Sri Lanka), Indonesia and India, a British businessman named John Dodd decided to make Taiwan his base for creating a unique brand of tea for the island to export. The brand was "Formosa Oolong" and since then Formosa tea has been synonymous with oolong tea. Prior to the 19th century, the people of Taiwan had been drinking and growing tea for a hundred years, since some of the plants had been brought from mainland China's Fujian Province.

Another milestone in tea production was the creation of a new type of tea on the island — pouchong. A lighter form of oolong, pouchong was developed in the small village of Pinglin in the late 1800s. It has since become one of the most sought-after teas in the world.

Tea drinking is ingrained into Taiwanese culture and there is a huge local market for Taiwanese teas, with large Taiwan-based tea brands supplying most of them. Taiwan is one of the few tea-producing regions in the world that imports more than double the amount it produces in order to keep up with local demand.

It is Taiwan we have to thank for the recent trend for bubble tea, also known as pearl milk tea — a tea-based drink that is often shaken with fruit or milk, with the addition of tapioca balls giving it its distinctive texture (see page 198).

CLIMATE, TERRAIN AND HARVESTING

Terrain is divided in Taiwan between flat coastal plains and high mountain regions but the whole island sits astride the Tropic of Cancer, providing the ideal tea-growing climate: hot and humid with plenty of rainfall. Teas are produced on both the breezy plains and on the mountainsides, with both climates and terrains bringing unique flavors and aromas to the resulting teas.

The highest-quality oolongs are grown in the mountainous areas, whereas the main commercial tea plantations are in Nantou County, which contribute nearly 85 percent of Taiwan's annual tea production.

PRODUCES: 16,425 tons (14,900 tonnes)

EXPORTS: 3,465 tons (3,145 tonnes)

IMPORTS: 32,960 tons (29,900 tonnes)

CONSUMES: 45,195 tons (41,000 tonnes)

ANNUAL CONSUMPTION PER PERSON:
3 lb. 12 oz. (1.7 kg)

REGIONS

Tea is grown in all 15 counties of Taiwan, not including its islands. Much of the tea production takes place in the central Nantou County. It is important to note that a mountain range runs down the center of Taiwan, spanning parts of Nantou, Chiayi, Taichung and Hualien, so in these areas there are often two distinct climates and terrains in which tea is grown.

TAIPEI (NORTH)

Tea type: Pouchong teas (Pinglin), green Dragon Well

Climate/terrain: Most northerly area for tea growing in Taiwan; northeastern monsoon keeps region cool, damp and misty at lower elevations of 650 to 1,650 ft. (200–500 m)

Location: Northern Taiwan

Plantations: Pinglin, Wenshan, Shenkeng, Nangang, Sanhsia

NORTH EAST

Tea type: Green tea, Oriental Beauty (hsinchu)

Climate/terrain: Northeastern monsoon keeps region cool, damp and misty on the lower-altitude plains but there is also a mountain range in Miaoli

Location: Northeastern Taiwan

Plantations: Miaoli, Hsinchu

CENTRAL

Tea type: Li shan oolong (Taichung), large-scale commercial black and green teas (Nantou), don ding oolong (Nantou)

Climate/terrain: Low altitude but mountainous terrain; considerably foggy climate most of the year

Location: Central Taiwan

Plantations: Nantou, Chiayi, Taichung and Yunlin

SOUTHERN

Tea type: Ali shan oolong (Chiayi)

Climate/terrain: Mountainous terrain and hot tropical climate

Location: Southern Taiwan, sits on the Tropic of Cancer

Plantations: Chiayi, Pingtung

Right: At the Assam Black Tea Plantation near Sun Moon Lake, the largest body of water in Taiwan, a woman takes in the scent of a handful of fresh tea leaves.

TYPES OF TEA GROWN IN TAIWAN

Pouchong is a lightly oxidized oolong nearer to green tea than black in taste. It has a stronger flavor than green tea as it is oxidized, but only 8 to 10 percent, so it isn't as heavy as regular oolong. Pouchong teas, meaning "wrapped" teas, were developed in Taiwan using the rolling methods learned from Fujian Province. Although some are now produced in mainland China also, Taiwanese pouchongs remain the gold standard as the highest quality in the world. Pouchong has a very mild, floral aroma, a slightly buttery, luxurious flavor and a light yellowish liquor.

POUCHONG (BAO ZHONG)

Region: Pinglin district, Taipei

Climate/terrain: Harvested April to May, for one or two days; most northerly area for tea growing in Taiwan; north-eastern monsoon keeps region cool, damp and misty at lower elevations of 650 to 1,640 ft. (200–500 m)

Processing methods: Partially oxidized (only 8 to 10 percent), twisted and dried in drums

Taste profile: Light, clean flavors with a floral aroma

DONG DING (TUNG TING)

Region: Nantou County

Climate/terrain: Mountains, continuous fog

Processing methods: Oolong tea production plus roasting over charcoal

Taste profile: Premium tea with sweet, roasted nut aroma

LI SHAN (HIGH MOUNTAIN) OOLONG

Region: Mount Li (Pear Mountain), Taichung County

Climate/terrain: High altitude (one of the highest-grown teas in the world at 8,200 ft./2,800 m); mountainous climate and terrain

Processing methods: Slow growth due to cloudy, foggy high mountain conditions; produced and harvested by hand in small, limited batches

Taste profile: Premium tea with smooth, sweet and rich complex flavor

DONG FANG MEI REN (ORIENTAL BEAUTY)

Region: Mount Li (Pear Mountain), Taichung County

Climate/terrain: High altitude (one of the highest-grown teas in the world at 8,200 ft./2,800 m); mountainous climate and terrain.

Processing methods: Uniquely harvested in the summer months when the tea jassid cricket (*Jacobiasca formosana*) is at its peak — this insect eats the edges of leaves, starting the oxidization process; high oxidization

Taste profile: Refreshing but flowery

BUBBLE TEA

One of the most recent trends to captivate the wider world of tea has been bubble tea — the milky, sweet tea-based drink shaken with chewy tapioca pearls and served with a jumbo plastic straw. The original recipe was created in Taichung in the 1980s.

HOW IS IT MADE AND SERVED

Traditionally, bubble tea is made with hot black tea, tapioca pearls and sweetened or condensed milk. The ingredients are shaken together to produce a thin layer of foam. However, many varieties of bubble tea have been invented, both hot and cold, using the addition of fruit syrups, flavored milks and even small pieces of fruit jelly instead of tapioca pearls. There is no end to the possible combinations of bubble tea, and this has made bubble-tea shops increasingly popular all over the world.

In a bubble-tea shop there is usually a shaker machine that mixes the bubble tea. The cup in which the tea is served is sealed with a layer plastic film or a lid, which is pierced with a drinking straw that is wide enough for the tapioca pearls to pass through.

Left: From its origins in Taiwan, bubble tea has become increasingly popular and there are now dedicated bubble-tea shops and bars all over the world, like this one in Los Angeles.

Opposite: Anything goes when it comes to flavorings, which range from fruit — this is a raspberry bubble tea — to chocolate, coffee, nuts and flowers.

VIETNAM

The fifth largest producer of tea in the world, Vietnam produces a wide variety of teas, including black, green, white and oolongs, but the domestic market is mainly for floral and scented green teas. Much like the Dutch in Indonesia and the British in India, the French led efforts to establish a tea industry in Vietnam in the 1800s.

Unfortunately, due to increasing conflict and destruction of lands suitable for tea cultivation, the industry didn't really take off there to the same level.

Today, the Vietnamese tea industry has huge potential for growth, as there are thousands of acres of suitable land still untouched. Interestingly, the tea trees growing along Vietnam's northern border, shared with China, are the oldest so far to be discovered.

Above: Tea grown at Tan Cuong village in Vietnam's northern province of Thai Nguyen is among the most highly valued green teas from this region.

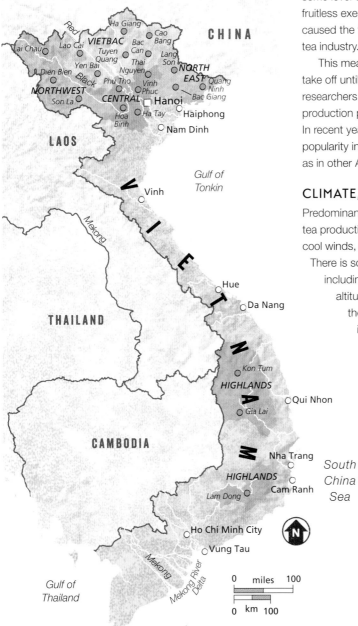

PRODUCES:	236,225 tons (214,300 tonnes)
EXPORTS:	161,710 tons (146,700 tonnes)
IMPORTS:	220 tons (200 tonnes)
CONSUMES:	79,335 tons (72,000 tonnes)

ANNUAL CONSUMPTION PER PERSON:
1 lb. 9 oz. (700 g)

HISTORY AND DEVELOPMENT

Although green tea has been enjoyed for many centuries in Vietnam, after first being introduced by the neighboring Chinese, it wasn't until the 1800s that commercial tea cultivation was established in the country, by the French colonialists who settled there.

The French set about producing black CTC teas in Vietnam, in an attempt to compete with the Dutch in Indonesia and the British in India and Sri Lanka. They also produced some green tea, with which they enjoyed some level of success, but this proved to be a somewhat fruitless exercise as the following years of war and unrest caused the total destruction of the fledgling Vietnamese tea industry.

This meant that the Vietnamese tea trade didn't really take off until much more recently. In the 1950s, Russian researchers helped Vietnam set up tea factories and production processes in return for favorable tea exports. In recent years Vietnamese tea has been growing in popularity in Europe, the United States and Russia as well as in other Asian countries.

CLIMATE, TERRAIN AND HARVESTING

Predominantly located in the northern mountain regions, tea production in Vietnam benefits from a tropical climate, cool winds, consistent rainfall and nutrient-rich soils. There is some variety in terrain from area to area, including both forested mountain regions and low-altitude plains, but the quality of Vietnamese tea on the whole remains at a high standard because of its ideal climate.

Production and harvesting methods developed under the funding and education of what was then the Soviet Union placed some key tea plantations in Vietnam at the forefront of tea production methods. However, following the collapse of the Soviet Union, this shift to plantation and factory methods slowed and today production is mainly completed by family-run farms where harvests take place three to four times a year.

The Tam Dao mountain range runs through three provinces, including Vinh Phuc, one of the regions of Vietnam where green tea grows.

REGIONS

NORTHWEST REGION

Tea type: Oolong teas

Climate/terrain: 1,640 ft. (500 m) altitude; mountain forest with cool airflow

Location: Northwest Vietnam, bordering Laos

Plantations: Son La, Lai Chau, Dien Bien

VIETBAC REGION

Tea type: Black, green, oolong and white teas

Climate/terrain: Mountain forests; warm but with cool winds

Location: Northern Vietnam, bordering China

Plantations: Ha Giang, Yen Bai, Tuyen Quang, Lao Cai, Bac Can, Cao Bang

NORTHEAST REGION

Tea type: Green teas

Climate/terrain: Mountain forests; warm but with cool winds

Location: Northeastern Vietnam, bordering China

Plantations: Quang Ninh, Lang Son, Bac Giang

CENTRAL REGION

Tea type: Green teas

Climate/terrain: Mountainous in parts, low-altitude plains in others; subtropical climate with monsoon seasonality

Location: North/central Vietnam

Plantations: Thai Nguyen, Phu Tho, Hoa Binh, Ha Tay, Hanoi, Vinh Phuc

HIGHLANDS REGION

Tea type: Oolong teas

Climate/terrain: Mountainous, 2,790 to 4,930 ft. (850–1,500 m); subtropical climate with cool mist and airflow

Location: Southern/central Vietnam

Plantations: Lam Dong, Gia Lai, Kon Tum

Below: Gathering to share early-morning tea in the atmospheric Old Town of the city of Hoi An, a popular tourist destination.

TYPES OF TEA GROWN IN VIETNAM

About a third of the tea produced in Vietnam is green, and much of it is scented. This tea is consumed domestically or by other South Asian countries. Vietnam's black teas are mostly CTC and destined for the blending export market. The remaining teas produced here are high-grown oolongs and white silver needle, often used to create flowering teas.

SHAN TUYET

Region: Bah Butong, Sumatra

Climate/terrain: High elevation — 6,560 ft. (2,000 m) — misty and moist; bright and long sunny days and nutrient-rich, red volcanic soil

Processing methods: Leaves plucked from wild-growing, ancient, tall tea trees rather than terraced, pruned bushes; lightly rolled and steamed before drying delicately

Taste profile: Sweet, fresh-tasting notes with smooth aftertaste

HIGH MOUNTAIN OOLONG

Region: Lam Dong, Central Highlands

Climate/terrain: High elevation — 3,280 ft. (1,000 m); forested mountainside with crisp airflow and misty seasonality bringing delicate aromas to the tea leaves.

Processing methods: Twenty percent oxidized and tightly twisted and rolled

Taste profile: Buttery oolong notes with a sweet, floral aftertaste

ARTICHOKE TEA

Although not a product of the tea plant, Vietnam produces a tea made from artichoke plants in the Lam Dong Highlands. It has a milky, sweet flavor and is very popular all over Vietnam, and Southeast Asia, for its health benefits.

NAM LANH

Region: Yen Bai, northern Vietnam

Climate/terrain: Mountainous region but tea terraces set into the valley hillsides near the Red River Delta; lush, well irrigated soil and tropical monsoon seasonality

Processing methods: Black tea processing with the addition of twisting prior to drying

Taste profile: Rich, malty, black tea, good with milk

JASMINE GREEN TEA

Region: Ha Giang Province (as well as other places), northern Vietnam

Climate/terrain: Tea terraces planted on the rolling, misty hillsides among the towering limestone mountains that help create mist and cool airflow.

Processing methods: Gently rolled and steam-dried, then scented with fresh jasmine blossom

Taste profile: Flavorsome, full green tea notes with sweet fragrant aroma of jasmine; bright and refreshing on the palate

DRAGONFLOWER BLOOMING TEAS

Hand-tied blooming teas, traditionally of Chinese origin, are popular in Vietnam. These little pearls of delicate, scented white or green buds are skilfully tied together and often have a flower blossom at their center. When placed in hot water these teas really do bloom, creating a wonderful floral flavor and a beautiful display. Vietnam now produces its own blooming teas, named dragonflower teas, made from luxury white silver needle tea.

LOTUS TEA (TRÀ SEN)

A Vietnamese specialty, lotus tea is made by scenting green tea with lotus flowers. It is often reserved for special occasions.

INDONESIA

This archipelago, spanning thousands of miles of the Indian and Pacific Oceans, is the eighth largest producer of tea in the world, with production mostly taking place on the two largest islands, Java and Sumatra. Indonesia was one of the earliest countries to be cultivated for tea after the Dutch East India Company took *assamica* bushes from India and planted them here in the 1600s. For many years Indonesia was a big global player in the black tea market, but the devastating effects of World War II slowed the pace. However, a recent revival, particularly focused on green tea production, has seen Indonesia's tea industry go from strength to strength. Indonesian teas, both green and black, are often used for blending, alongside African, Ceylon and Indian teas.

Above: Tea plantations have flourished on Java since Jacobus Jacobson planted tea bushes here in the 1800s.

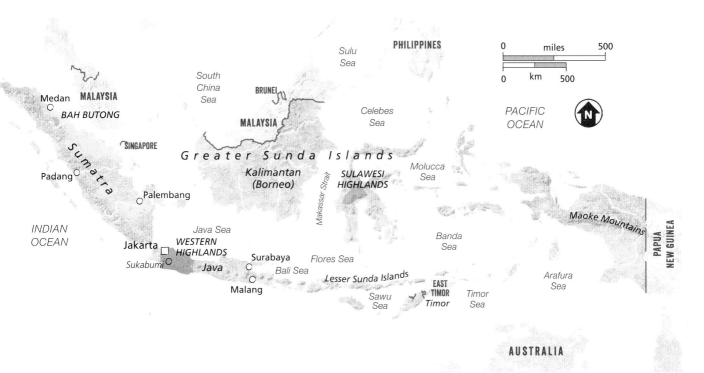

HISTORY AND DEVELOPMENT

In the 1600s the Dutch East India Company set up business on Java to ship spices, tea and other goods back to Europe from the Far East. For many years, the company controlled all imports and exports in Indonesia and so could easily facilitate the import of Chinese tea plants. The initial efforts of one Dutchman, Jacobus Jacobson, to cultivate tea on Java soon led to the stark realization that the *sinensis* variety of tea bushes were not at all suited to the tropical climate. So, instead, he decided to try the *assamica* variety that was doing so well for the British over the sea in India, and these plants immediately thrived in the island's mineral-rich soil.

Throughout the 18th and 19th centuries, tea production flourished, as there was a high demand for Indonesian black teas in Europe. So production spread out from Java to a neighboring island, Sumatra, and then on to Sulawesi. Before World War II, Indonesia was the fourth largest producer of tea in the world and its teas were held in the highest regard. But the war brought great destruction to the Indonesian tea industry, both in terms of infrastructure and of labor, and it has been fighting hard to get back on top ever since.

PRODUCES: 163,140 tons (148,000 tonnes)

EXPORTS: 77,240 tons (70,070 tonnes)

IMPORTS: 26,895 tons (24,395 tonnes)

CONSUMES: 104,433 tons (94,740 tonnes)

ANNUAL CONSUMPTION PER PERSON: 13 oz. (380 g)

CLIMATE, TERRAIN AND HARVESTING

Terrain varies dramatically across Indonesia's thousands of islands but tea plantations have mostly thrived in the rich volcanic soil found in the forested, mountainous areas. The tropical climate is predominantly stable and there is plenty of rainfall at the higher altitudes, so the bushes can be harvested all year long. The best harvests are between July and September.

Since the devastation of World War II, Indonesia has put a lot of resources into replanting and repairing tea plantations and upgrading equipment and machinery.

REGIONS

Tea is grown across 13 provinces in Indonesia:

WESTERN HIGHLANDS, JAVA

Tea type: Taloon black tea

Climate/terrain: Highland rainforest with seasonal monsoon; hot and humid

Location: West Java, near Bogar and Bandung

Plantations: Malabar, Ciater, Wallini, Cibuna, Cisaruni, Kerasarie

SUKABUMI, JAVA

Tea type: Black tea, complex and fruity

Climate/terrain: Higher altitude, more than 2,000 ft. (600 m); misty with cool breeze and rainy seasonality; tea terraces planted on the flat plains at the foot of the mountain terrain

Location: West Java

Plantations: Goalpara, Nirmala

SULAWESI HIGHLANDS, SULAWESI

Tea type: Black tea, green tea both for export and blending market

Climate/terrain: Tropical jungle terrain but cool climate; the foggy, rainy season hits the tea terraces

Location: South Sulawesi, Gow District

Plantations: Malino

TYPES OF TEA GROWN IN INDONESIA

Described as light, aromatic and full of flavor, Indonesian teas are regularly compared to high-grown Ceylon teas. Most black tea is used for black breakfast tea blends and most green tea is used for average-grade teabags. It is unusual to find many single-estate Indonesian teas, but the country does produce a small amount of oolong.

There is a decent demand for Indonesian tea from the local market, where it can be found blended and packaged in the supermarket or at tea stalls at the roadside.

BAH BUTONG

Region: Bah Butong, Sumatra

Climate/terrain: High elevation — 6,560 ft. (2,000 m); misty and moist, bright and long sunny days and nutrient-rich, red volcanic soil

Processing methods: Orthodox tea, mostly BOP grades produced during many sifting stages

Taste profile: Strong, dark body and color with floral notes

TALOON

Region: Bandung, West Java

Climate/terrain: 6,235 ft. (1,900 m); cool air and rocky soil

Processing methods: Orthodox tea production

Taste profile: Said to be Indonesia's highest-quality tea, an aromatic and flavorful infusion with golden tips

Opposite: This photograph from the 1930s shows Javanese women sorting through baskets of dried tea to remove twigs and other debris.

JAPAN

Japan was one of the earliest countries to cultivate tea. In the eighth century Buddhist scholars discovered tea while studying in China and brought it back home to Japan, where it was first grown for its medicinal uses and only later celebrated for its spiritual and ceremonial properties. This was long before tea grew in popularity to become a staple for the whole nation.

Today, Japan ranks tenth in the world in terms of tea production, and fourth in tea consumption. For centuries, tea was grown at the foot of the mountains near Uji, a city south of Kyoto, by Buddhist monks, but now plantations can be found all over Japan. The biggest tea-producing region is Shizuoka, which is responsible for nearly half of Japan's tea. It is also common for tea grown elsewhere in

---

Above: Most of the tea grown in Shizuoka, home to Mount Fuji — Japan's highest peak — is sencha green tea.

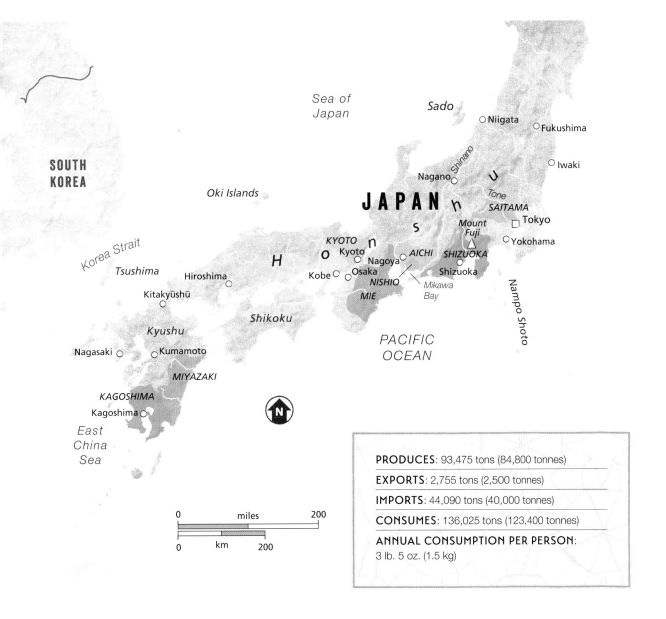

Sea of Japan

Sado

○ Niigata

○ Fukushima

SOUTH KOREA

Oki Islands

Shinano

Nagano○

○ Iwaki

JAPAN

Tone

SAITAMA

□ Tokyo

Mount Fuji

○ Yokohama

Korea Strait

Tsushima

H   O

KYOTO

○ Kyoto

AICHI

SHIZUOKA

Hiroshima ○

Kobe ○

Nagoya ○

○ Osaka

NISHIO

○ Shizuoka

Mikawa Bay

Kitakyūshū ○

MIE

Shikoku

PACIFIC OCEAN

Nampo Shoto

Kyushu

Nagasaki ○   ○ Kumamoto

MIYAZAKI

KAGOSHIMA

Kagoshima ○

East China Sea

N

	miles	
0		200
0	km	200

PRODUCES: 93,475 tons (84,800 tonnes)

EXPORTS: 2,755 tons (2,500 tonnes)

IMPORTS: 44,090 tons (40,000 tonnes)

CONSUMES: 136,025 tons (123,400 tonnes)

ANNUAL CONSUMPTION PER PERSON: 3 lb. 5 oz. (1.5 kg)

Japan to end up in Shizuoka for processing. Two things all Japanese tea plantations share are a relatively close proximity to the ocean and the use of distinct steaming methods, so their teas are always easily recognized by their fresh, grassy and vegetal flavors.

HISTORY AND DEVELOPMENT

Japanese people consume a vast amount of tea, which is not surprising, considering how closely it is woven into all spheres of society and culture, playing a huge part in ceremony, medicine, hospitality and spiritual customs. Quite a remarkable feat when you consider that the tea plant isn't even native to Japan.

Tea was first cultivated in Japan in the eighth century in the grounds of Buddhist temples, nestled in the foothills of the Uji mountains. After visiting China, where *Camellia sinensis* was a native species and already popular as a beverage, Buddhist scholars were impressed with the medicinal qualities of green tea and so took tea seeds back home to Japan. The earliest mention of tea in Japanese literature dates to 815 CE, when tea was recorded as being served to Emperor Saga. Tea remained rare, valuable and available only to the imperial court for many centuries that followed.

In the 12th century, the Zen Buddhist monk Eisai wrote a treatise called *Kissa Yojoki* (*How to Stay Healthy Drinking Tea*) about the medicinal benefits of drinking tea, as a result of which plantations began to spring up in Kyoto to produce tea for spiritual and health purposes. Tea leaves were steamed, dried and ground into a fine powder, called matcha. Its high antioxidant levels saw it become popular with both Samurai warriors in battle and Buddhists undergoing training.

Tea didn't make the transition from medicine to beverage in Japan until the 14th century, when the tea ceremony was developed; *sado* or *chado*, as it is called in Japan, became the art of hospitality through tea. The tea ceremony became very fashionable, spreading through the upper classes and traveling merchants. By the 15th century it had become an everyday occurrence in the streets of Japan.

In the 17th century, the Dutch East India Company began to export tea from Japan to Europe and later to the United States, and tea soon became Japan's main export commodity. This resulted in the Japanese government engaging in trade treaties, developing mechanization and providing flat land for plantations.

CLIMATE, TERRAIN AND HARVESTING

Most Japanese tea is grown on small farms that share a communal factory. It is just as common to find the odd tea field nestled among urban houses and by the side of busy roads as it is to find fields in the remote mountains.

The climate differs depending on region, but in general it is warm and moist, because of the location next to the sea or by rivers. There are two types of growing methods: in sunlight or under canopy, with some bushes being shaded just a few weeks before harvesting (see page 61).

There are three or four harvests a year in Japan, sometimes five in milder climates. But the sought-after first

THE UJI METHOD

Invented in the 18th century to produce sencha and bancha, the Uji method of processing tea saw demand for these types of tea explode both in Japan and abroad. Developed by a tea farmer in the mountains near Uji, the new method involved steam-drying and hand-rubbing the leaves, replacing traditional pan-roasting techniques. This new method created the very fresh and fragrant taste so distinct to Japanese tea. Later it became possible to replicate this method using machinery and sencha and bancha remain Japan's most popular tea types to this day.

flush is in April, with June and September being the usual months for standard cuttings. The earlier in the season the tea has been harvested, the higher the quality. At this stage, pickers are looking for the top two leaves and the shoot of the plant, but for later harvests they may turn to the slightly lower leaves, geared to producing a different type of tea. By suiting their tea production to time of harvest, Japanese tea farmers are able to maximize their yearly yield.

It is very rare to find any organic tea production in Japan as demands on the climate, soil and plants because of the limited number of harvests each year mean that chemicals have always been used to enhance the harvest. The result can be that export potential is restricted as some countries do not find the levels of chemicals used acceptable.

REFRIGERATING TEA

Because of the freshness of many of Japan's highest-quality green and oolong teas, it is important that they are sold and consumed quickly. The seasonal nature of harvesting in Japan can make this a challenge, especially as teas harvested at the very beginning of the year command higher prices. In order to manage their resources, many Japanese tea farmers put their processed teas into cold storage to keep them fresh. This is not the same as a domestic fridge, where too much oxygen and food aromas would damage the leaves, but, rather, a very carefully controlled specialized cold room or box designed specifically for maximizing the freshness of tea.

REGIONS

SHIZUOKA

Amount: Above 33,070 tons (30,000 tonnes)

Tea type: Mostly sencha

Climate/terrain: Flat plains; mild climate, with variable weather and rain; good quality water

Location: At the foot of Mount Fuji, near to Tokyo and major ports on the Pacific coast, so perfect for export

Plantations: Honyama, Makinohara, Kawane, Tenryu, Kakegawa

KAGOSHIMA

Amount: 28,660 tons (26,000 tonnes)

Tea type: Sencha, bancha and gyokuro

Climate/terrain: Flat plains; milder climates, warm and humid so longer harvests

Location: On southern island of Kyushu

Plantations: Saga, Miyazaki, Satsumacha, Fukuoka

MIE

Amount: Above 7,715 tons (7,000 tonnes)

Tea type: Mainly Kabuse-cha sencha

Climate/terrain: Mild climate; low altitude

Location: Central Japan, Honshu island

Plantations: Isecha

MIYAZAKI

Amount: Above 4.410 tons (4,000 tonnes)

Tea type: Sencha

Climate/terrain: Mountainous terrain with misty, cool climate

Location: On southern island of Kyushu

Plantations: Miyazakicha

KYOTO

Amount: Above 3,305 tons (3,000 tonnes)

Tea type: Gyokuro and sencha

Climate/terrain: Hilly terrain; damp, subtropical, mild in winter and humid in the summer

Location: Central Japan, Honshu Island

Plantations: Wazuka, Minami-Yamashiro, Uji

SAYAMA

Amount: 2,205 tons (2,000 tonnes)

Tea type: Sayama (sweet, rich, roasted tea)

Climate/terrain: Rain-drenched, lightly forested hills with cool climate, sometimes frost over winter

Location: Northwest of Tokyo

Plantations: Iruma

NISHIO

Amount: 2,205 tons (2,000 tonnes), 320 tons (290 tonnes) of matcha (25 percent of the national production)

Tea type: Matcha

Climate/terrain: Mild climate, misty air and rough terrain because of the Yahagi River; fertile soil

Location: Near the coast of Mikawa Bay, Honshu Island

Plantations: Aiya, Shimoyama

Right: Tea is harvested using a tractor at a tea plantation in Chiran, Kagoshima Prefecture.

TYPES OF TEA GROWN IN JAPAN

There are a variety of green teas produced in Japan, the most popular being bancha, sencha, gyokuro and tencha — the last used to make matcha. The most sought-after is the very first harvest, which happens on just one day in April and is used to produce shincha tea.

Japanese teas tend to be very grassy, oceanic and vegetal in flavor due to the consistent misty and moist climate. They can also be quite sweet to taste and full of complex flavors. Japanese tea tasters often describe a fifth taste — *umami* — which is hard to describe in English but the word translates to "a pleasant savory taste" (see page 56). It's often described as slightly salty, and this savory taste is also found in foods such as broth, miso and mushrooms.

GYOKURO

Region: Kyoto, Nishio

Growing conditions: Shaded canopy

Processing methods: "Uji" method — steamed, dried and kneaded

Taste profile: Fresh, fragrant, sweet, pale jade color

TENCHA

Region: Kyoto, Nishio

Growing conditions: Shaded canopy

Processing methods: Steamed, dried and ground. Flat leaf used — never rolled

Taste profile: Sweet, mellow, bright green

SHINCHA

Region: Shizuoka

Growing conditions: Sunlight, mild climate, mist and rain

Processing methods: Steamed 30 seconds, then sun-dried before "Uji" method of kneading

Taste profile: The rarest, sweetest, most sought-after first harvest of the year

SENCHA

Region: Shizuoka, Kyoto, Kagoshima

Growing conditions: Sunlight, mild climate

Grade: First and second flush; top three leaves

Processing methods: Steamed 30 seconds, then sun-dried before "Uji" method of kneading

Taste profile: Light and sweet, mellow, golden yellow color

BANCHA

Region: Shizuoka, Kyoto, Kagoshima

Growing conditions: Sunlight, mild climate

Grade: Third or fourth flush; larger lower leaves and some stems

Processing methods: Steamed 60 seconds, then sun-dried before "Uji" method of kneading

Taste profile: Mild taste, more astringent than sencha and distinctive straw aroma

HOJICHA

Region: Shizuoka, Kyoto, Kagoshima

Growing conditions: Sunlight, mild climate

Grade: Third or fourth flush; larger lower leaves and some stems

Processing methods: Steamed 30 seconds, then sun-dried before "Uji" method of kneading; additional roasting

Taste profile: Fresh but flavorful, roasted notes similar to black teas; dark, almost red, in color

Opposite: Entitled *The First Tea of the Year*, this 1816 woodcut by Katsushika Hokusai (1760–1849) shows two women and a child at a tea party.

Tea growing in built-up urban areas is a common sight in Japan, with bright-green rows of neatly trimmed tea plants sitting side-by-side with homes, roads and railway tracks.

MATCHA TEA CEREMONY

The traditional Japanese tea ceremony continues to be much revered in Japanese culture. Originally performed by the Samurai warrior class, it centers upon the ceremonial act of preparing and serving matcha tea. The movements involved, and the spiritual meaning behind them, is called the Way of Tea and was developed by followers of the Zen school of Buddhism.

MATCHA TEA

Matcha is a high-quality powdered green tea made from the youngest buds of the tea plant (see page 56). The buds are plucked during the spring, then ground using a mill stone to a fine powder. Two types of tea are used in the tea ceremony. *Koicha* ("thick tea"), which is heavy and almost souplike, is shared from the same bowl, thereby reflecting and respecting the unity of the group. *Usucha* ("thin tea") is enjoyed at the end of the ceremony in individual cups while guests converse with one another. Both teas are commonly enjoyed alongside Japanese sweets, which serve both to line the stomach and to complement and contrast with the bitter notes of the tea.

THE CEREMONY

A typical tea ceremony lasts 3 to 4 hours and consists of many elements, including two types of tea, lunch, sweets and often a break in the garden.
1. Greeting **2.** Lunch **3.** Garden **4.** Thick tea
5. Sweets **6.** Thin tea **7.** Good-bye

EQUIPMENT

Each guest must bring three items to the tea ceremony – a fan, a small square of Japanese paper and a knife. The fan should be one that is never used for practical or decorative reasons, only for the tea ceremony. At the beginning of the ceremony each person places their fan in front of them and bows to the group, in silence, as a respectful act of greeting. The Japanese paper is used as a napkin or plate on which to place the traditional sweets served as part of the ceremony, and the small knife is used to cut the sweets.

The host will wear a traditional kimono, and will also have a traditional handkerchief, used to purify and cleanse all equipment before and after use. The tea ceremony takes place on the floor, which is covered with bamboo mats, called *tatami*. No shoes must be worn on the tatami, by guests or by the host, which serves to remind the guests of their proximity to simplicity and nature, and of their respect for the occasion.

The host will choose their most beautiful tea bowls and present them to their guests with the decorative design at the front. Before they drink, each guest will turn the bowl clockwise two turns, to show the beautiful design to the host. This is to show respect for their host and to ensure that they drink only from the back of the bowl.

A matcha tea scoop, called *chashuku*, is used to measure and transport the matcha to the bowl. Tea scoops are true works of art, often crafted and named by the tea masters themselves. The master will choose a name that reflects nature and the seasons and that sends a message that they wish to pass on during the ceremony. The tea container, used for storing the matcha powder, may also have a message or design that encourages reflection in this way.

ZEN SPIRITUALITY

For Zen Buddhists tea is more than a hot beverage; it is the opportunity to pause and reflect, to be quiet and still, and to contemplate spiritual enlightenment. There are four elements of spirituality to be remembered during the tea ceremony: harmony, purity, respect and tranquility. Every action and movement performed in the ceremony has a spiritual meaning, even the guests' manner of entering the tea room: the door is often very low so guests must bow down or even crawl to get in. This is to remind us to be humble and respectful of others and the world around us.

Opposite: *Sado*, or the Way of Tea, is as much about ceremony, ritual and aesthetics, as it is about matcha, the powdered green tea that is served.

THAILAND

Tea was introduced to Thailand by the Chinese, both through centuries of trade and by Chinese settlers in northern Thailand. The knowledge, skills and techniques developed in mainland China and, later, on the island of Taiwan were used to establish the production of oolong and green teas in Thailand. The same ancient tea trees grow in the forests in the mountains of northern Thailand that grow in northern Vietnam, spanning a vast area from Assam in India to Yunnan in China. It is no surprise, then,

that Thai teas are known for their high quality. They are also usually organically grown.

The most common Western notion of Thai tea is of a milky, sweet, black tea, served iced, but this drink does

---

Above: A holiday resort set on a tea plantation near Ban Rak Thai, a village close to Thailand's border with Burma (Myanmar), famed for both its breathtaking scenery and tea cultivation.

not in fact originate from Thailand, but was probably introduced from Europe or America. It is also usually made with Ceylon tea rather than Thai tea. That said, it remains popular in Thailand today.

HISTORY AND DEVELOPMENT

The oldest tea plants were discovered in the forests of northern Thailand, where they have grown for thousands of years. Thai hill tribes would, and still do, use the fresh leaves to make a hot beverage by boiling them in water, as well as eating the leaves in various meals.

Early tea cultivation mostly took place in the far north of the country, where a melting pot of cultures lived together in the infamous Golden Triangle. Although Thailand's neighbors were trying to use force to change the area's affiliation with the illegal opium production and trade, King Bhumibol Adulyadej (1927–) knew that this approach would not to work. He recognized that the opium trade supported the livelihoods of thousands of tribespeople and knew he must offer them an alternative product to cultivate if he was to succeed. So cultivating tea became the answer, the various peoples in the area already having the knowledge and skills required from time spent working on tea gardens in China and Vietnam.

Tea cultivation continued to grow in other areas and in the 1960s another influx of Chinese refugees flooded the northern settlements of Chang Mai and Chang Rai. They were welcomed to settle in the region but tasked with setting up more commercially viable tea production. So they had to rely on Taiwanese tea plants, which had been developed to produce oolong teas.

CLIMATE, TERRAIN AND HARVESTING

The climate in northern Thailand, where most tea is produced, is dictated by the monsoon weather pattern. This creates three seasons — wet, dry and rainy — with warm temperatures all year round. The tea plants can only be harvested during the warmer months but these span all the seasons and the best teas are said to be harvested during the monsoons.

PRODUCES: 82,675 tons (75,000 tonnes)	
EXPORTS: 1,655 tons (1,500 tonnes)	
IMPORTS: 6,175 tons (5,600 tonnes)	
CONSUMES: 85,980 tons (78,000 tonnes)	
ANNUAL CONSUMPTION PER PERSON: 2 lb. 7 oz. (1.1 kg)	

REGIONS

CHANG RAI

Tea type: Oolong, green and black teas, pu'erh (in Doi Wawee)

Climate/terrain: 5,900 ft. (1,800 m) altitude, mountainous and thick forest; tropical and humid

Location: Northern tip of Thailand, bordering Laos

Plantations: Doi Mae Salong, Doi Wawee, Doi Tung, Doi Chang

CHANG MAI

Tea type: Oolong, green and black teas

Climate/terrain: 4,625 ft. (1,400 m) altitude, mountainous and thick forest; tropical and humid

Location: Northern tip of Thailand, bordering Burma (Myanmar)

Plantations: Doi Pu Muen

MAE HONG SON

Tea type: Oolong teas

Climate/terrain: Deep valley; misty almost all year

Location: Northwest Thailand, bordering Burma (Myanmar)

Plantations: Ban Rak Thai

SHAN TEA

Thailand's northern mountains and forests are home to the Shan tribespeople, as well as to some of the oldest wild tea trees in the world. The Shan people who settled in these forests mostly came from Yunnan, China. There are many groups within the Shan people, some living on the Thai side, some in Burma (Myanmar), Laos and Vietnam. In the 19th century, after a battle for independence with the Burmese government, there was a big migration of Shan people into Thai towns such as Chang Rai, Chang Mai and Lampang.

Called Tai Yai by Thai people, the Shan tribespeople have been growing, harvesting and drinking tea in various forms for many years. Their knowledge and labor helped to shape the Thai tea industry as it is known today. The Shan people of Pang Kham, in Mae Hong Son Province, produce traditional pu'erh tea that is almost all enjoyed locally but is starting to gain some recognition within Southeast Asia.

TYPES OF TEA GROWN IN THAILAND

Green and oolong teas are grown in Thailand.

OSMANTHUS OOLONG TEA

Region: Doi Mae Salong in the north

Climate/terrain: High elevation — 5,900 ft. (1,800 m); misty cool air circulates in the mountains and cooler temperatures slow growth and develop flavor

Processing methods: Semi-oxidized and hand-twisted oolong, then the traditional Chinese method of scenting leaves with *Osmanthus fragrans* flowers

Taste profile: Vibrant, luxurious mouthfeel with floral blossom flavors and smooth, rich notes

---

JIN XUAN BLACK TEA

Region: Doi Mae Salong in the north

Climate/terrain: High elevation — 5,900 ft. (1,800 m); misty cool air circulates in the mountains and cooler temperatures slow growth and develop flavor

Processing methods: Fully processed black tea, sometimes rolled

Taste profile: Deep red color, nutty and malty with aromatic notes

---

Right: The second largest province in Thailand, the mountainous northern province of Chiang Mai produces green, black and oolong teas.

SOUTH AMERICA

Tea production is possible in the warmer countries of South America, with Argentina in particular contributing a high amount of the world's exports. The standard of tea here isn't high enough to warrant any demand for single-estate or specialty teas, but teas from all over South America are great for use in black tea blends or in the iced and instant teas that are popular in North America. There is a large market in South America for yerba mate, which is sometimes considered a herbal tea and used as a blending ingredient. This is the preferred hot beverage in Argentina, Bolivia, Uruguay and Brazil. The Amazon rainforest is rich in cultivation and biodiversity and many herbal tea-blending ingredients are harvested there, particularly those with stimulating properties, such as mate, guayusa and guarana.

TEA-PRODUCING COUNTRIES

(IN ORDER OF PRODUCTION VOLUME)

ARGENTINA

Argentina is the only country from this region to produce tea on a large commercial scale. Most of Argentina's teas are black and used for blending.

Produces: 115,745 tons (105,000 tonnes)
Exports: 85,980 tons (78,000 tonnes)
Imports: 330 tons (300 tonnes)
Consumes: 4,520 tons (4,100 tonnes)
Annual consumption per person: 3½ oz. (100 g)
Tea profile: Low-quality, unbranded black teas used for blending, iced and instant tea export markets

PERU

Tea in Peru is mostly grown around the high-altitude Cusco region. Although the country has dabbled in exporting tea, there isn't much demand, so the black tea produced in Peru is destined for the domestic market, where tea is served sweet and black. In the mountains of Cusco, there is also a large demand for locally grown coca tea, as it is supposed to help with altitude sickness. This tea is derived from the same plant, *Erythroxylum coca*, that is used to produce cocaine.

Produces: 4,760 tons (4,320 tonnes)
Exports: None
Imports: 660 tons (600 tonnes)
Consumes: 3,750 tons (3,400 tonnes)
Annual consumption per person: 3½ oz. (100 g)
Tea profile: Low-grade black teas for domestic market

ECUADOR

Black teas are also produced in Ecuador, where the quality is higher than in other South American countries and the flavors tend to be stronger.

Produces: 3,305 tons (3,000 tonnes)
Exports: 660 tons (600 tonnes)
Imports: 55 tons (50 tonnes)
Consumes: 2,205 tons (2,000 tonnes)
Annual consumption per person: 5 oz. (140 g)
Tea profile: Strong, full-bodied teas with malty notes

Previous pages: A tea plantation near Panambí in the province of Misiones. The region is relatively flat, which allows for mechanized harvesting.

COLOMBIA

Quito □
ECUADOR
Guayaquil ○

Iquitos ○
Amazon

PERU

A n d e s
Ucayali

Trujillo ○

Callao □
Lima □
Cuzco ○

Arequipa ○
Lake Titicata

PACIFIC
OCEAN

BOLIVIA

BRAZIL

PARAGUAY

Salta ○

CHILE

A n d e s

ARGENTINA

Córdoba ○

Paraná
Uruguay

Rosario ○

URUGUAY

Buenos
Aires □

Colorado

Bahía Blanca ○

ATLANTIC
OCEAN

A n d e s

Patagonia

0   miles   600
0   km   600

N

PRODUCES: 127,535 tons (115,700 tonnes)

EXPORTS: 108,467 tons (98,400 tonnes)

IMPORTS: 191,140 tons (173,400 tonnes)

CONSUMES: 220,495 tons (200,030 tonnes); nearly 1,102,310 tons (1,000,000 tonnes) if yerba mate included

ANNUAL CONSUMPTION PER PERSON: 1 lb. 2 oz. (500 g)

227

ARGENTINA

Argentina is the only nation from the Americas to feature among the top 10 tea-producing countries in the world. Although Argentina is vast, neither the country's terrain nor its climate are, for the most part, suitable for tea growing. Small pockets of ideal conditions exist in the tropical northeastern areas of Misiones and Corrientes. Argentina produces black teas that are strong in flavor and perfect for adding body to blends. In China and North America, two of Argentina's biggest export markets, the black teas

are also used for iced or instant tea blends. Because of this and the fact that the domestic market prefers drinking yerba mate to tea, it is very rare to find any single-estate or specialty Argentinian teas.

Above: Transporting yerba mate leaves from a plantation in Santo Pipó, Misiones. A member of the holly family, yerba mate is considered the national beverage of Argentina — more popular with the local population than tea.

HISTORY AND DEVELOPMENT

Yerba mate, a plant similar to tea, had already been cultivated and consumed in Argentina for hundreds of years before tea was introduced to the country from the Soviet Union in the 1920s. Local yerba mate farmers were encouraged to try growing tea alongside their other crops as an additional revenue stream. However, the low quality of the tea produced and the lack of local demand meant that, initially, tea wasn't regarded as a viable crop as it didn't command high prices.

By the 1950s the Argentinian government had placed a ban on imported teas so local demand helped boost tea cultivation once again. The introduction of mechanized harvesting and processing techniques also helped increase productivity in the industry.

CLIMATE, TERRAIN AND HARVESTING

The climate and terrain of Misiones and Corrientes make these two regions the only areas suitable for growing tea in Argentina. The climate is subtropical, hot and humid, and tea is harvested only during the summer months, between November and May.

Although there are currently still a number of smaller tea farms, Argentina's tea industry is dominated by large estates, which produce black teas for blending at a large scale. Because of local labor shortages and the relatively low quality of the tea produced here, both harvesting and the factories are heavily mechanized.

Tea type: Black tea for blending market
Climate/terrain: High, flat lands; subtropical climate and consistent rainfall
Location: Misiones and Corrientes, northeast
Processing methods: CTC black tea produced for the export blending market

PRODUCES: 115,745 tons (105,000 tonnes)

EXPORTS: 85,980 tons (78,000 tonnes)

IMPORTS: 330 tons (300 tonnes)

CONSUMES: 4,520 tons (4,100 tonnes)

ANNUAL CONSUMPTION PER PERSON: 3½ oz. (100 g)

YERBA MATE

Argentina produces and consumes a large amount of yerba mate. A species of the holly (Aquifoliaceae) family, this plant has a much longer history in Argentina than tea. It has been cultivated and enjoyed by Amazonian tribespeople for hundreds of years for its naturally stimulating properties.

Yerba mate is usually prepared in a hollowed-out gourd and sipped through a metal straw called a *bombilla*. The bombilla has an enclosed end with small holes that act as a filter to ensure that one drinks the hot beverage rather than the leaves themselves. It is customary for Argentinians to carry this mate-making equipment with them, along with a thermos of hot water in order to enjoy and share yerba mate all day long.

In the 21st century mate can still be considered the national beverage and nearly 220,500 tons (200,000 tonnes) of it are consumed by Argentinians each year. Mate is cultivated under similar climate conditions and in the same areas of Argentina as tea, but, unlike tea, this crop is mostly produced for the domestic market.

Top, left: Argentinian gauchos, or cowboys, like this modern-day one, have always relied on yerba mate to sustain them as they herd their cattle.

Top, right: This yerba mate plantation is in Misiones, a province in northeastern Argentina where a good proportion of the country's tea harvest is also grown.

Bottom, left: Although mate is traditionally served in a hollow gourd with a metal drinking straw, these days mate cups also come in a range of contemporary patterns and styles.

Bottom, right: Yerba mate is enjoyed throughout Central and South America, including Argentina, Bolivia, Brazil, Uruguay and Paraguay.

GLOSSARY

Biodiversity
A contraction of "biological diversity," this term refers to all levels of plant and animal life on the planet in its natural environment.

Black tea
Dark brown and higher in caffeine than other varieties, black tea is the most common variety and accounts for 80 percent of the tea consumed in the Western world.

Blend
This refers to different teas mixed together to produce a final product – English breakfast and Russian caravan, for example. It also refers to mixing tea with non-tea ingredients, such as flowers or herbs. Masala chai is an example. *See also* Scenting, Inclusions

Caffeine
A natural stimulant found in tea, the levels of which vary depending on where the tea is grown and how it is processed. Generally speaking, more processed teas contain higher levels of caffeine but this is not always so.

CTC
Short for Crush, Tear, Curl. This is when tea leaves are cut and torn in to smaller pieces during processing, and then rolled and curled into pellet-type particles.

Dust
The smallest particles of tea leaf and lowest grade of tea.

Estate *see* Plantation.

Fannings
Finely broken pieces of tea leaf that still have a recognizable coarse texture; they are the grade of tea used in most teabags.

Farm
A tea farm is run by an individual, assisted by family, and sometimes by other workers in the community. Farmers will sell their harvested tea leaves to a nearby plantation or factory to process

Firing *see* Killing the green.

First drying *see* Killing the green.

Fixing the green *see* Killing the green.

Flush
Some teas are identified by the flush, or plucking season, during which they are harvested. Considered the highest quality, the first flush is between February and May.

Grade
This refers to the grade of the leaf when plucked. It is also used to refer to the size of processed tea-leaf particles.

Green tea
Unlike other types of tea, green tea undergoes an additional early drying stage to halt oxidization and preserve its green, leafy appearance and inhibit the development of caffeine. *See also* Gyokuro

Gunpowder tea
Green tea that consists of tiny rolled pellets, said to resemble gunpowder.

Gyokuro
A Japanese green tea that is cultivated in shade, rather than sun. *See also* Green tea.

Inclusions
Ingredients such as dried berries that can be added to a tea blend for their aesthetic or health-giving properties but do not affect the tast profile.

Killing the green
A heating process that deactivates enzymes in the tea leaf to halt oxidization; also called "fixing the green," "firing" and "first drying."

Masala chai
Black tea blended with spices such as peppercorns, ginger, cardamom and cinnamon, brewed in milk and sweetened. It is widely drunk throughout India.

Matcha
Finely ground green tea powder that is used in the traditional Japanese tea ceremony.

Mouthfeel
A term used to describe the texture of tea during drinking.

Oolong tea
A traditional Chinese tea that is partially oxidized. It is more complex in taste than green tea but not as strong as black tea.

Orange pekoe
Orange pekoe are medium-grade whole black tea leaves of a specific size. It is often abbreviated to "OP."
See also Pekoe.

Orthodox
This refers to the whole leaf or the particles of the whole leaf, rather than CTC.

Oxidization
The process in which the cell walls of tea leaves break down, changing their chemistry, due to an enzymatic reaction with oxygen

Pearled tea
These teas, which include jasmine pearls and dragon pearls, are tea leaves hand-rolled into pearl-sized balls that unravel when they are steeped in hot water.

Pekoe
A term used in some countries as part of the grading system for black tea.

Plantation
Also called an estate, this is a large tea-growing area under the control of a central organization.

Plucking
Harvesting tea leaves by hand is known as plucking and is the traditional method of collecting the leaves for processing.

Pu'erh tea
Pu'erh tea is packed into cakes or bricks and left to mature. To drink it, a small amount is crumbled from the cake or brick. Pu'erh tea is grown in Yunnan, China.

Rolling
Part of the processing stage, this involves pressing leaves to squeeze out moisture and break down the cells in the leaves.

Scenting
Flavor notes can be added by exposing tea leaves to fresh blossoms during processing, or by blending the tea with dried flowers or essential oils later.

Tannins
Polyphenols, which are naturally occurring compounds in tea with a bitter, astringent flavor.

Taster
Tea companies have experienced and trained in-house tasters responsible for tasting every batch of tea to make sure that the flavor and quality remain consistent.

Tisane
A fruit or herbal tea. Tisanes do not contain tea leaves but are often produced and brewed in the same way.

Traceability
The ability to track a product through all stages of production, processing and distribution.

Variety
This refers to the different forms that the tea leaf can take after processing – black, white, green, etc. are all varieties of tea.

White tea
This is the least processed variety of tea; the leaves are often simply plucked and then gently dried.

Withering
Drying tea leaves by causing water to evaporate from them using either a natural breeze or withering fans. Some teas are withered in sunlight.

INDEX

Page references for illustrations are in *italics;* major references are in **bold**

PICTURE CREDITS

Alamy age fotostock 55 above; Alison Teale 120; Alissa Everett 196; blickwinkel/Koenig 17; Bo Løvschall 195; Christian Guy/Hemis 230 above; David Noton Photography 158; dbimages 148; Dinodia Photos 15; FLPA 46 below; Heritage Image Partnership Ltd 82 center; Hugh Threlfall 83 left; imageBROKER 178; Imagestate Media Partners Limited - Impact Photos 231 below; ipm 89; Japan Stock Photography 216; Jason Rothe 228; Kirsty McLaren 56; Michele Burgess 54; Michele Falzone 163 below; Neil Cooper 132; Patrizia Wyss 176; Roger Bamber 160; Simon Rawles 52, 69; TAO Images Limited 163 above; The Artchives 81; Tomeu Ozonas 224; ton koene 134 above; Tuul and Bruno Morandi 42, 156; Xinhua 184.

Bridgeman Images © Tyne & Wear Archives & Museums 29; Pictures from History 61. **Corbis** Mark Lance/Aurora Photos 35; Everett Kennedy Brown/epa 58; Harry Choi/TongRo Images 75 above left; Hugh Sitton 152; Jiang Kehong/Xinhua Press 53 above; Keren Su 213; Le-Dung Ly/SuperStock 180; Pete Mcbride/National Geographic Creative 146; R. Ian Lloyd/Masterfile 154; Tuul and Bruno Morandi 45.

Dreamstime.com Aerogondo 171 right; Beijing Hetuchuangyi Images Co. Ltd. 192; Kritchanut 40; Nui7711 41; Sandman 231 above; Vladyslav Danilin 170 below; Yulianta Ramelan 206.

Getty Images Sasha 73; Alfred Eisenstaedt/ullstein bild via Getty Images 94; Ali Kabas 172; APIC 189; Ariadne Van Zandbergen 124; Art Media/Print Collector 30; Ashit Desai 204; Ashok Sinha 170 left; Belisario Roldan 75 below left; Benson/Fox Photos/Hulton Archive 76; Danita Delimont 168; DEA Picture Library 83 center; DeAgostini 82 right; Evans/Three Lions 209; Florilegius/SSPL 13; General Photographic Agency 38; hsvrs 18; Hulton Archive 78; Ishara S. Kodikara/AFP 157; J. A. Hampton/Topical Press Agency 8; Jerry Redfern/LightRocket via Getty Images 46 above; John S Lander/LightRocket via Getty Images 219; JTB Photo/UIG via Getty Images 14,

210; Kenneth Shelton/EyeEm 198; London Stereoscopic Company 62; Mike Copeland 2; Museum of East Asian Art/Heritage Images 82 left; Nathalie Bardin/AFP 139 above; Nigel Pavitt 130; Pam McLean 75 below right; Popperfoto 37; Prashanth Vishwanathan/Bloomberg via Getty Images 55 below; Quynh Anh Nguyen 202; Rob Whitrow 75 above right; Sanjit Das/Bloomberg via Getty Images 26, 97; Scott Robertson 115; Simon Murrell 83 right; Thierry Falise/LightRocket via Getty Images 53 below; Tim Draper 93; Trevor Snapp/Bloomberg via Getty Images 136; VisitBritain/Andrew Pickett 101.

iStockphoto.com aphotostory 190; danishkhan 7; kvkirillov 175; Lauri Patterson 199; Lokia 194; Maximova 149; narvikk 134 below; omersukrugoksu 108; pattonmania 164; piccaya 230 below; Teradat Santivivut 223.

Library of Congress 63, 214.

Mary Evans Picture Library Retrograph Collection 92; The National Archives 91.

Reuters Mike Hutchings 139 below; Nguyen Huy Kham 200; Thomas Mukoya 128.

REX Shutterstock Design Pics Inc 86; Geoff Pugh 105; imageBROKER 47; Majority World 140, 144.

Shutterstock feiyuezhangjie 186; Songkris Khunkham 220.

SuperStock DeAgostini/DeAgostini 167.

TopFoto ullsteinbild 21.

Wellcome Library, London 188.

AUTHOR'S ACKNOWLEDGMENTS

I want to thank Shamal and family as well as his team at Tea-Link, Colombo for all their help and hospitality out in Sri Lanka.

To the team at Obubu Tea, who let me take part in their award-winning Shincha harvest in Wazuka.

To Ayumi and family for their incredible hospitality and knowledge of organic Japanese tea farming.

A big thank you to my partner in crime, business and life, Mike, who has patiently been on hand to help, especially during the all-nighters.

To my family and friends, particularly Teabird Andi, who have all shared in my excitement and pride in fulfilling a lifelong ambition of writing a book.